Apache 2
Pocket Reference

WITHDRAWN

1 6 APR 2022

Apache 2
Pocket Reference

Andrew Ford

O'REILLY®

Beijing · Cambridge · Farnham · Köln · Sebastopol · Taipei · Tokyo

Apache 2 Pocket Reference
by Andrew Ford

Copyright © 2008 Ford & Mason Ltd. All rights reserved.
Printed in Canada.

Published by O'Reilly Media, Inc., 1005 Gravenstein Highway North, Sebastopol, CA 95472.

O'Reilly books may be purchased for educational, business, or sales promotional use. Online editions are also available for most titles (*http://safari .oreilly.com*). For more information, contact our corporate/institutional sales department: 800-998-9938 or *corporate@oreilly.com*.

Editor: Simon St.Laurent
Copy Editor: Katie Nopper DePasquale
Production Editor: Loranah Dimant
Proofreader: Loranah Dimant
Indexer: Lucie Haskins
Cover Designer: Karen Montgomery
Interior Designer: David Futato

Printing History:

    September 2008:   First Edition.

ISBN: 978-0-596-51888-2

[TM]

1221153506

Contents

Preface

Apache is a powerful web server designed with a modular architecture to be both efficient and portable. It is extremely flexible, offering the ability for a single server to support multiple websites as virtual hosts and to act as a web proxy. Apache includes standard modules for caching, to support SSL/TLS connections, various authentication and authorization mechanisms, and a filtering system. There are many add-on modules that extend Apache's functionality providing features, such as templating engines, embedded interpreters for many scripting languages, and HTTP interfaces to systems such as the Subversion version control system.

This pocket reference summarizes Apache's command-line options and the configuration directives for the modules in the standard distribution. It covers Apache version 2.2.9, but most information is applicable to any version of Apache 2. For comprehensive information, the scale of which is beyond the scope of a small guide such as this, the Apache documentation website (*http://httpd.apache.org/docs/*) should be your next point of referral.

Conventions

The following conventions are used in this book:

`constant width text`
> Denotes literal text.

`constant width italic text`
> Denotes dummy parameters.

`{ A | B }`
> Denotes alternatives.

`[text]`
> Denotes optional text.

`...`
> Indicates that the previous element may be repeated.

Using Code Examples

This book is here to help you get your job done. In general, you may use the code in this book in your programs and documentation. You do not need to contact us for permission unless you're reproducing a significant portion of the code. For example, writing a program that uses several chunks of code from this book does not require permission. Selling or distributing a CD-ROM of examples from O'Reilly books does require permission. Answering a question by citing this book and quoting example code does not require permission. Incorporating a significant amount of example code from this book into your product's documentation does require permission.

We appreciate, but do not require, attribution. An attribution usually includes the title, author, publisher, and ISBN. For example: "*Apache 2 Pocket Reference* by Andrew Ford. Copyright 2008. Ford & Mason Ltd., 978-0-596-51888-2."

If you feel your use of code examples falls outside fair use or the permission given above, feel free to contact us at *permissions@oreilly.com*.

Safari® Books Online

 When you see a Safari® Books Online icon on the cover of your favorite technology book, that means the book is available online through the O'Reilly Network Safari Bookshelf.

Safari offers a solution that's better than e-books. It's a virtual library that lets you easily search thousands of top tech books, cut and paste code samples, download chapters, and find quick answers when you need the most accurate, current information. Try it for free at *http://safari.oreilly.com*.

How to Contact Us

Please address comments and questions concerning this book to the publisher:

> O'Reilly Media, Inc.
> 1005 Gravenstein Highway North
> Sebastopol, CA 95472
> 800-998-9938 (in the United States or Canada)
> 707-829-0515 (international or local)
> 707 829-0104 (fax)

We have a web page for this book, where we list errata, examples, and any additional information. You can access this page at:

To comment or ask technical questions about this book, send email to:

> *bookquestions@oreilly.com*

For more information about our books, conferences, Resource Centers, and the O'Reilly Network, see our web site at:

http://www.oreilly.com

Acknowledgments

I would like to thank all my reviewers, especially Chris Pepper and my wife, Catherine Mason, who both did sterling work; my colleagues at MessageLabs for their support; the staff at O'Reilly—in particular my editor, Simon St.Laurent, and Abby Fox, who turned my ideas about how the book should be typeset into reality; and finally all of the Apache developers, the Apache HTTPD project, and the countless individuals who have contributed to make Apache what it is and keep on improving it.

CHAPTER 1

Introduction

This chapter gives an overview of the architecture of Apache, how to obtain the software, starting and stopping the server, and the basics of configuration files.

Architectural Overview

Apache is normally run as a system daemon or service, with a parent process or thread supervising a number of child processes or threads that perform the request processing. Apart from certain core features, most functionality is implemented by modules, which may be either statically linked into the server or dynamically loaded on startup.

Operating systems vary in how they implement features such as networking and multiprocessing. Apache version 2.0 introduced MultiProcessing Modules (MPMs) to provide networking and scheduling models tailored to particular operating systems and usage patterns, as listed in Table 1-1. MPMs use the native features of the operating system and provide scheduling using processes, threads, or a mix of the two. Apache uses only a single MPM at any time, and it must be statically compiled into the server.

Table 1-1. MultiProcessing modules

Module	Description
beos	Mutithreaded MPM for the BeOS operating system
event	Experimental variant of the *worker* MPM
mpm_netware	Threaded MPM for Novell Netware
mpm_winnt	Twin process, multithreaded MPM for Windows
mpmt_os2	Hybrid multiprocess, multithreaded MPM for O/S2
prefork	Traditional nonthreaded, preforking MPM
worker	Hybrid multiprocess, multithreaded MPM

The MPMs, other modules, and the core web server build upon the Apache Portable Runtime (APR), which provides a consistent, platform-independent interface to the underlying operating system. APR includes APIs to access SQL databases and LDAP servers; these are used in two framework modules, *mod_dbd* and *mod_ldap*, which provide common facilities that other modules may use.

Operational Overview

On startup, Apache goes through an initialization stage before entering its operational state. During the initialization stage, Apache reads and verifies its configuration files, opens network connections and log files, acquires system resources, and creates the pool of child processes or threads that will handle requests. Apache is normally started with **root** privileges but relinquishes those privileges before it enters the operational state.

Once Apache has entered its operational state, the child processes or threads handle incoming requests. Requests are processed in a number of phases, and each phase provides a number of hooks for modules to participate in the processing. For each hook, Apache calls registered functions in turn until they have all been called or until one of them indicates either that processing for that hook is complete or that an error has occurred.

Modules register handlers for the phases during which they need to influence the handling of the request. Generally, a module only registers handlers for one or two phases.

The phases occur in the following order:

Request parsing
> The request URL is mapped into the filesystem namespace.

Security controls
> Access control, authentication, and authorization rules are applied.

Request preparation
> The request URL and mapped file path are matched against the configuration to determine the content handler and any filters to use, and to set other metadata.

Content generation
> Runs the chosen content handler with any filters.

Request logging
> Logs the request.

This picture is complicated slightly by the fact that modules can issue subrequests to return a document other than the one requested, or to check what the response would be if a request was made for a different resource.

Current Versions of Apache

At the time of this writing (summer 2008), there are three major versions of Apache in common use: 1.3, 2.0, and 2.2.

Apache 1.3 was released in June 1998 and for many years was the most widely used web server. Work started in 2000 on a new architecture for Apache; the first production release of the new version, Apache 2.0, was made in April 2002. At the same time, a new version-numbering scheme was introduced: odd numbered minor versions, such as 2.1 or 2.3, are development versions; even numbered minor versions, such as 2.0 or 2.2, are stable versions. The first 2.2 release was made in November 2005, and the latest point release, 2.2.9, was made in July 2008.

The Apache website includes documentation on the changes between versions and notes on upgrading.

How to Obtain Apache

The Apache web server is available for most modern computing platforms—most Linux and BSD distributions offer it as a standard package, and it is included in Mac OS X. Binary packages for Microsoft Windows are available from the Apache website and its mirrors, as are source and other binary packages. It is advisable to familiarize yourself with the particulars of the distribution you deploy, as packagers invariably change details to conform with the conventions of their target platform.

Alternatively, compiling Apache from source is quite straightforward, and has the advantage of giving complete control over how it is built, which modules are statically included in the server, and so on. The source distribution includes instructions on the build process.

By default, the source distribution installs into the subdirectories listed in Table 1-2 under */usr/local/apache2*. Most third-party distributions use variations on this scheme.

Table 1-2. Layout of standard Apache directories

Directory	Contents
bin	Program files (administrative program files are often placed in an *sbin* directory).
build	Files used by the apxs utility.
cgi-bin	CGI scripts.
conf	Configuration files (often stored in the */etc* directory hierarchy).
error	HTTP error messages in multiple languages.

Directory	Contents
htdocs	HTML documents.
icons	Icon image files.
include	C language include files needed for compiling third-party modules.
logs	Log files and runtime status files, such as the PID file; however, status files are often stored in a *run* directory.
man	Manual pages (often stored in the system *man* directories).
manual	A local copy of the Apache manual.
modules	Loadable modules.

Apache distributions include a number of modules and utility programs; these are listed in Appendix A.

Starting and Stopping Apache

Most packaged distributions of Apache arrange for the server to be started automatically when the system is booted, and stopped when the system is halted.

On Unix-like systems, Apache normally runs as a daemon process. A shell script, `apachectl`, is included with Apache to automate the process of starting and stopping the daemon. This script is usually invoked by a system startup script. Apache will respond to the following signals sent to the parent process (the process ID of which is stored in the PID file):

TERM

> Stops the server by causing the parent process to attempt to kill each of the child processes and then terminate itself.

HUP

> Restarts the server by causing the parent process to kill off each of the child processes, reread the configuration files, and then spawn new child processes. Server statistics are reset to zero on a restart.

USR1

> Initiates a graceful restart. Child processes exit either after processing the current request or immediately if not currently serving a request. The parent process rereads the configuration files and starts to spawn new child processes to maintain the appropriate number of server processes. Server statistics are not reset on a graceful restart.

WINCH

> Initiates a graceful stop. Child processes exit either after processing the current request or immediately if not currently serving a request. The parent process removes the PID file and stops listening on all ports, but continues monitoring until any remaining children have exited or the timeout has expired.

On Windows, if Apache was installed as a service, it can be started and stopped with the NET START and NET STOP commands with the Apache Service Monitor.

Command-Line Options

Should you need to start Apache manually, the server program takes the following command-line options:

-C *directive*

> Processes *directive* before reading configuration files.

-c *directive*

> Processes *directive* after reading configuration files.

-d *directory*

> Sets the initial value for ServerRoot.

-D *parameter*

> Defines a parameter that can be used in <IfDefine> sections. Certain startup options are invoked by setting parameters (DEBUG, FOREGROUND, NO_DETACH, ONE_PROCESS).

-E *filename*

> Sets the error log file for server startup.

-e *level*

> Sets the log level for server startup.

-f *file*

Main configuration file (default is *conf/httpd.conf*).

-h

Prints a short help message containing a summary of the command-line options.

-k *command*

Executes one of the following commands: **start**, **restart**, **graceful**, **stop**, or **graceful-stop**. Also, on Windows only: **install**, **uninstall**.

-L

Lists available configuration directives (provided by compiled-in modules) and exits.

-l

Lists compiled-in modules and exits.

-M

Lists compiled-in and shared modules and exits (equivalent to **-D DUMP_MODULES**).

-n *name*

Windows only: service name for Apache.

-S

Shows virtual host settings (equivalent to **-D DUMP_VHOSTS**).

-t

Tests the syntax of configuration files, checking for the existence of document root directories, and exits.

-v

Prints version and build date and exits.

-V

Shows compilation settings and exits.

-w

Windows only: keeps the console window open after Apache has started.

-X

Runs in single-process debug mode (equivalent to **-D DEBUG**).

Configuration Files

Every aspect of Apache's behavior is controlled by directives stored in its configuration files. When Apache starts or restarts, it first reads the main server configuration file from the default location, or from the location specified with the -f command-line argument. Further configuration files may be included with the Include directive.

Configuration files are plain text files that contain configuration directives, blank lines, and comments. Leading whitespace on a line is ignored, as are blank lines. Lines starting with a hash sign (#) are regarded as comments.

Configuration Directive Format

Apache configuration directives are described in a standard format as shown here.

DirectorySlash	SVDH (Indexes)
mod_dir (B)	ON

DirectorySlash { ON | OFF }

Compatibility: 2.0.51 and later

If set to ON, then requests that map to a directory but that do not end in a trailing slash will be redirected to the same URL with a trailing slash appended, enabling automatic directory indexes and relative URLs to work correctly.

The top line gives the name of the directive on the left, and the list of contexts in which the directive may be used on the right, using the abbreviations defined in Table 1-3. If the directive can be used in a per-directory configuration file and is controlled by an AllowOverride directive category, the category keyword is included in parentheses after the context abbreviations.

Table 1-3. Context abbreviations

Context	Description
S	Valid in global context, i.e., in the server configuration files outside of any virtual host or filesystem container sections
V	Valid in virtual host sections
D	Valid in directory-type container sections (`<Directory>`, `<Files>`, `<Location>`, and the *Match variants)
H	Valid in per-directory configuration file (named *.htaccess* by default)
*	Indicates that the directive may be given more than once in a context

The second line lists the name of the Apache module that implements the directive on the left (see Appendix A for a list of the modules included in the Apache distribution) with the status of the module in brackets, using the abbreviations from Table 1-4. The module may be listed as "MPM," in which case the MPMs implementing the directive will be noted, or as "core" to indicate that the directive is implemented by the Apache core module. The default value for the directive is shown on the right.

Table 1-4. Module status codes

Status	Description
B	Base module—included in the Apache distribution and compiled-in by default
E	Extension module—included in the Apache distribution but not compiled-in by default
X	Experimental module—included in the Apache distribution but not compiled-in by default

The next line gives the directive syntax, followed by compatibility notes if relevant. Directives are case-insensitive, as are most arguments that do not refer to case-sensitive objects such as filenames.

Basic Configuration File Directives

These directives control where configuration files are located, which additional files are loaded at startup, the name of the per-directory configuration files, and which directives are allowed in those files.

ServerRoot S

core   depends on compilation settings

ServerRoot *directory*

Root directory for the server. May be overridden with the -d command-line option. Relative paths for other directives, such as Include and LockFile, are interpreted as being relative to this directory. Binary packages often have different defaults from the standard Apache layout.

Include SVD*

core

Include { *filepath* | *directory* }

Compatibility: wildcard matching available in 2.0.41 and later

Reads and processes the contents of the named configuration file, which is logically included in place of the directive. The filename part of the path may include shell-style wildcard characters, in which case, all matching files are included in lexicographical order. If a directory is specified, then all files in the directory and any subdirectories are included, which is not recommended, as it may pick up unintended files.

AccessFileName SV*

core   .htaccess

AccessFileName *filename* ...

Names the per-directory configuration file. Although the directive name and default value imply otherwise, the file is not restricted to access control directives. The AllowOverride directive controls which directives are allowed.

```
AllowOverride category ...
```

The **AllowOverride** directive is only allowed in non-regular expression **<Directory>** sections. It specifies whether per-directory configuration files are read for directories matched by the section and for subdirectories of those directories—and, if read, which of the categories of directives listed in Table 1-5 are allowed in those files. If a per-directory configuration file contains directives that are not allowed, an internal server error is generated.

Table 1-5. Per-directory override categories

Category	Meaning
None	Per-directory configuration files are not read at all.
All	All directives are valid in per-directory configuration files.
AuthConfig	Authentication and authorization directives.
FileInfo	Directives controlling document attributes.
Indexes	Directory indexing directives.
Limit	Access control directives.
Options	Directory features.

An **AllowOverride** directive replaces any settings defined for higher-level directories. The keywords **All** and **None** are parsed in the same way as the other keywords, which allows some strange but valid combinations.

Conditional Sections

Conditional sections enclose blocks of directives that Apache should ignore while parsing the configuration files if the condition specified on the section start directive is not met. Conditional sections may be nested.

<IfDefine> SVDH*

core

```
<IfDefine [!]parameter >
    ...
</IfDefine>
```

Enclosed directives are only evaluated if the named parameter is defined with the -d command-line option—or is not defined if *parameter* is preceded by an exclamation mark (!).

<IfModule> SVDH*

core

```
<IfModule [!]module >
    ...
</IfModule>
```

Enclosed directives are only evaluated if the specified module is active—or inactive if *module* is preceded by an exclamation mark (!). Modules can be specified by their identifier or by their name, including the trailing ".c" as printed by the -l command line. The use of module identifiers was introduced in version 2.0. This directive can be used to differentiate between 1.3 and the newer version, as the core module is named core.c as of 2.0; in 1.3, it was http_core.c.

<IfVersion> SVDH*

mod_version (E)

```
<IfVersion [[!]operator] major[.minor[.patch]] >
    ...
</IfVersion>
```

Compatibility: 2.0.56 and later

Enclosed directives are only evaluated if the Apache version matches the specified criteria. If the *patch* and *minor* version number components are omitted, they are taken as zero. The comparison operator can be one of the following: =, <, <=, >, or >= (== is a synonym for =).

Regular expression matching is also supported: you can use the ~ operator and specify the version as a string, or use the = operator and specify the version as */regex/*.

All operators may be preceded by an exclamation mark (!) to reverse their meaning.

Container Sections

Container sections allow the scope of directives to be limited by directory, filename, URL, or request method. The `<Directory>`, `<DirectoryMatch>`, `<Files>`, and `<FilesMatch>` directives introduce filesystem containers, while the `<Location>` and `<LocationMatch>` directives introduce webspace containers. `<Limit>` and `<LimitExcept>` introduce container sections limited by request method.

The non-`*Match` filesystem and webspace container directives each take a shell wildcard pattern argument. These directives have an alternative form in which the first argument is specified as a literal tilde (~) followed by a second argument that is interpreted as a regular expression. This form is exactly equivalent to the corresponding `*Match` directives, which should be preferred, as the tilde is easy to overlook.

Shell wildcard patterns may contain metacharacters and bracket expressions: ? matches a single character; * matches any number of characters; and [*expr*] matches any of the characters, or ranges of characters, enclosed between the brackets.

When processing a request, directives within filesystem and webspace sections are applied in the following sequence:

1. Non-regular expression `<Directory>` sections and per-directory configuration files, working from shortest to longest pathname. The per-directory configuration files override the `<Directory>` sections.

2. `<DirectoryMatch>` sections.

3. `<Files>` and `<FilesMatch>` sections.

4. `<Location>` and `<LocationMatch>` sections.

Directives in `<Directory>` and `<DirectoryMatch>` sections and per-directory configuration files apply to subdirectories unless overridden later.

Container sections for a matching virtual host are applied after those for the main server.

<Directory>   SV*

core

```
<Directory pattern >
    ...
</Directory>
```

Container for directives that apply only to directories that match the specified pattern (and their subdirectories).

<DirectoryMatch>   SV*

core

```
<DirectoryMatch regex >
    ...
</DirectoryMatch>
```

Enclosed directives apply only to directories (and their subdirectories) that match the specified regular expression.

<Files>   SVDH*

core

```
<Files pattern >
    ...
</Files>
```

Enclosed directives apply only to files that match the specified filename pattern.

<FilesMatch>   SVDH*

core

```
<FilesMatch regex >
    ...
</FilesMatch>
```

Enclosed directives apply only to files that match the regular expression.

`<Location>` SV*

core

```
<Location pattern >
   ...
</Location>
```

Enclosed directives apply only to URLs that match the specified pattern.

`<LocationMatch>` SV*

core

```
<LocationMatch regex >
   ...
</LocationMatch>
```

Enclosed directives apply only to matching URLs.

`<Limit>` SVDH*

core

```
<Limit method ... >
   ...
</Limit>
```

Enclosed directives apply only to matching methods.

`<LimitExcept>` SVDH*

core

```
<LimitExcept method ... >
   ...
</LimitExcept>
```

Enclosed directives apply to nonmatching methods.

CHAPTER 2

Server Environment

This chapter discusses how the server environment is configured, including the setup of virtual hosts, networking, and process scheduling. It also covers the new framework modules, *mod_dbd* and *mod_ldap*. These provide interfaces to the SQL database and LDAP APIs of APR, thus removing the need for every module that accesses a database or LDAP server to provide its own code to do so.

Main Server and Virtual Hosts

Apache is configured with the `Listen` directive to listen on multiple IP addresses on one or more ports. Without any virtual host definitions, all requests will refer to the main server.

Virtual hosts are defined using `<VirtualHost>` sections, but these have an effect only if Apache is listening on the IP address and port specified on the opening `<VirtualHost>` directive. If no `NameVirtualHost` directive is specified, all virtual hosts are based on IP address.

`NameVirtualHost` directives are used to designate IP addresses with optional port numbers that will accept requests for the name-based virtual hosts—hostnames can be used instead of IP addresses. Apache determines the virtual host to be used by matching the value of the `Host` header on requests arriving on these IP addresses and ports against the server name or the aliases defined in virtual host sections where the address and port on the <VirtualHost> directive exactly match the values on the NameVirtualHost directive. Note that name-based virtual hosts do not work with HTTPS connections, because the hostname is needed to set up the secure connection but can only be extracted from the HTTP headers once the connection has been set up.

<VirtualHost>   S*

core

```
<VirtualHost addr[:port] ... >
    ...
</VirtualHost>
```

Container for directives that apply only to a particular virtual host. *addr* may be an IP address or the fully qualified domain name for the virtual host; it may also be the literal _default_, which will match any IP address not explicitly listed in another virtual host section. A port number can be specified with *port*. Both *addr* and *port* may be specified as * to match any address or port respectively.

For name-based virtual hosts, if there is no section that matches on ServerName or ServerAlias, and there is no section that uses _default_, then the <VirtualHost> section that is defined first will be used.

NameVirtualHost   S*

core

```
NameVirtualHost addr[:port]
```

Sets the IP address for subsequent name-based virtual host sections.

ServerAdmin   SV

core

```
ServerAdmin { email-addr | URL }
```

Email address or URL included in error messages generated by Apache.

ServerAlias V*

core

ServerAlias *fqdn* ...

Alternative names for a host used with name-based virtual hosts.

ServerName SV

core

ServerName [*scheme://*]*name*[*:port*]

Hostname and port to use when creating redirection URLs. If not set, the hostname is determined automatically by DNS lookup on the IP address, and the port of the incoming request will be used. See also UseCanonicalName.

ServerPath V

core

ServerPath *pathname*

URL path for pre-HTTP 1.0 clients that do not send a Host header. Requests that start with this path will use the current virtual host.

ServerSignature SVDH
OFF
core

ServerSignature { ON | OFF | Email }

Controls the generation of a footer line containing the server address on server-generated documents, such as error responses and directory listings. If set to Email, the email address set with the ServerAdmin directive is included as a mailto: link.

ServerTokens S
Full
core

ServerTokens *level*

Controls the level of detail returned in the Server response headers.

Prod[uctOnly]
    Product name only, e.g., Apache

Major

> Product name and major version number, e.g., `Apache/2`

Minor

> Product name, and major and minor version number, e.g., `Apache/2.2`

Min[imal]

> Product name and full version number, e.g., `Apache/2.2.9`

OS

> Product name, full version number, and operating system, e.g., `Apache/2.2.9 (Debian)`

Full

> Product name, full version number, operating system, and information about compiled-in modules, e.g., `Apache/2.2.9 (Debian) mod_ssl/2.2.9 OpenSSL/0.9.8g`

UseCanonicalName   SVD

core   OFF

`UseCanonicalName { ON | OFF | DNS }`

If set to `ON`, Apache uses the server name and port specified with the `ServerName` directive when constructing self-referential URLs and setting the `SERVER_NAME` and `SERVER_PORT` environment variables. If set to `OFF`, Apache uses the server name specified in the `Host` header (if specified) and the port on which the connection was made. If set to `DNS`, Apache performs a reverse DNS lookup on the IP address to which the connection was made to determine the server name; then Apache uses the port on which the connection was made.

UseCanonicalPhysicalPort   SVD

core   OFF

`UseCanonicalPhysicalPort { ON | OFF }`

If set to `ON`, the server will never consider the physical port, i.e., the port that the request is received on, when constructing self-referential URLs.

Network Configuration

Apache listens for requests on the network ports specified with `Listen`. There are a number of parameters that can be changed to optimize the performance of the network connection.

AcceptFilter   S*

core

`AcceptFilter` *protocol filter*

Enables operating system-specific optimizations for `accept()`.

AcceptMutex   S
MPM   default

`AcceptMutex { default | method }`

Compatibility: event, prefork, worker

Method used to serialize the acceptance of requests on network sockets. The available methods and their relative performance varies across platforms, and are listed in Table 2-1.

Table 2-1. Methods for AcceptMutex

Method	Description
default	Uses the default selected at compile-time
flock	Uses the `flock` system call to lock the file defined by the `LockFile` directive
fcntl	Uses the `fcntl` system call to lock the file defined by the `LockFile` directive
posixsem	Uses POSIX-compatible semaphores to implement the mutex
pthread	Uses POSIX mutexes as implemented by the POSIX Threads (PThreads) specification
sysvsem	Uses System V-style semaphores to implement the mutex

EnableSendfile
SVDH (FileInfo)

core   ON

`EnableSendfile { ON | OFF }`

Compatibility: 2.0.44 and later

Controls whether the `sendfile()` system call is used for transmitting file contents to the client. This feature can be used when the server does not need to inspect the data within the file, but, in certain circumstances, it may be better to disable it.

HostnameLookups
SVD

core   OFF

`HostnameLookups { ON | OFF | Double }`

Controls whether DNS lookups are performed to resolve hostnames for logging and passing to CGI and SSI scripts. If set to `double`, following each successful reverse DNS lookup, a forward lookup is performed to check that the IP address matches the hostname. Regardless of the setting, access controls based on hostname will always use a double DNS lookup.

KeepAlive
SV

core   ON

`KeepAlive { ON | OFF }`

Enables persistent connections, which allow a network connection to be reused for subsequent requests by the same client, thus avoiding the overhead of establishing separate connections.

KeepAliveTimeout
SV

core   15

`KeepAliveTimeout seconds`

Timeout for subsequent requests on a persistent connection.

MaxKeepAliveRequests

S
100

core

MaxKeepAliveRequests *number*

Maximum number of requests that can be processed on a persistent connection. A value of zero is taken to mean no limit.

Listen

S*

MPM

Listen [*IP-addr:*]*port-number* [*protocol*]

Compatibility: all MPMs (required since 2.0)

Specifies the network port and address on which the server listens for connections. The *protocol* argument is new in version 2.1.5 and defaults to http for port 80 and https for port 443.

ListenBacklog

S
511

MPM

ListenBacklog *number*

Compatibility: all MPMs

Maximum number of entries for the operating system's listen queue of pending connections. If connection requests arrive faster than Apache can process them, the queue will overflow. The OS will reject further requests while the queue remains full.

ReceiveBufferSize

S
0

MPM

ReceiveBufferSize *nbytes*

Compatibility: all MPMs

Sets the size of the TCP receive buffer; zero means to use the OS default.

SendBufferSize

S
operating system defaults

MPM

SendBufferSize *nbytes*

Compatibility: beos, mpm_netware, mpm_winnt, mpmt_os2, prefork, worker

Sets the size of the TCP send buffer; zero means to use the OS default.

Timeout   S

core   300 seconds, i.e., 5 minutes

`Timeout` *secs*

Timeout used for three purposes: receiving a request once a connection is accepted, between receipt of packets in the case of POST or PUT requests, and between acknowledgment packets when sending the response.

TraceEnable   S

core   ON

`TraceEnable { ON | OFF | Extended }`

Compatibility: 2.0.55 and later

By default, HTTP `TRACE` requests are allowed; if set to `OFF`, a 405 (Method Not Allowed) error is returned to the client. The `Extended` value is used for testing; see the Apache documentation for further details.

Win32DisableAcceptEx   S

MPM

`Win32DisableAcceptEx`

Compatibility: mpm_winnt in version 2.0.49 and later

Disables the use of `AcceptEx()` WinSock API for accepting network connections, and instead uses `accept()`. This may be used if third-party virus or networking products interfere with `AcceptEx()`.

Process Management

Apache uses a pool of child processes, threads, or a combination of the two to handle requests. Each MPM implements a slightly different model that plays to the strengths of the underlying operating system. In all models though, there is one process or thread that monitors the other request-handling processes or threads, increasing and reducing the pool size according to the current request load. The directives in this section provide controls over the maximum and minimum pool size, and other process management tuning parameters.

GracefulShutDownTimeout   S

MPM   0

`GracefulShutDownTimeout secs`

Compatibility: event, prefork, worker

Number of seconds the server should continue running, handling the existing connections, once a "graceful stop" signal has been received. If set to zero, the server will wait until all remaining requests have finished.

MaxClients   S

MPM   256

`MaxClients number`

Compatibility: beos, event, prefork, worker

Maximum number of child server processes that may be started, which thus limits the maximum number of requests that can be processed simultaneously.

MaxMemFree   SVDH*

MPM   0

`MaxMemFree kbytes`

Compatibility: beos, event, mpm_netware, mpm_winnt, prefork, worker

Maximum amount of free memory in kbytes that the memory allocator is allowed to hold without calling **free()**; zero means unlimited.

MaxRequestsPerChild   S

core   0

`MaxRequestsPerChild number`

Compatibility: event, mpm_netware, mpm_winnt, mpmt_os2, prefork, worker

Maximum number of connections that are processed by a child server process before it terminates voluntarily. Child processes may also terminate if the load drops. A value of zero is taken as unlimited. Setting this parameter can ameliorate the effect of memory leaks in servers, especially if *mod_perl* or other resource-hungry modules are used, as it can prevent runaway processes consuming all memory.

MaxRequestsPerThread

MPM	0

`MaxRequestsPerThread` *number*

Compatibility: beos

Maximum number of requests that an individual server thread will handle before exiting; zero means no limit.

MaxSpareServers

MPM	10

`MaxSpareServers` *number*

Compatibility: prefork

Maximum number of idle child server processes that may exist. If the server load drops, then the parent process will signal excess idle processes to terminate.

MaxSpareThreads

MPM	depends on MPM

`MaxSpareThreads` *number*

Compatibility: beos, event, mpm_netware, mpmt_os2, worker

Maximum number of idle threads. Default values are *beos*: 50; *mpm_netware*: 100; *mpmt_os2*: 10; *event* and *worker*: 250.

MaxThreads

MPM	2,048

`MaxThreads` *number*

Compatibility: mpm_netware

The number of threads allowed.

MinSpareServers S

MPM   5

`MinSpareServers` *number*

Compatibility: prefork

Minimum number of idle child server processes that should be present. If the number drops below this level, the parent process will create new child processes to maintain a pool of processes that is ready to accept new connections.

MinSpareThreads S

MPM   depends on MPM

`MinSpareThreads` *number*

Compatibility: BeOS, event, mpm_netware, mpmt_os2, worker

Minimum number of idle threads. Defaults values are *beos*: 1; *mpm_netware*: 10; *mpmt_os2*: 5; *event* and *worker*: 75.

ServerLimit S

MPM

`ServerLimit` *number*

Compatibility: event, prefork, worker

Upper limit on configurable number of processes. Default is 256 for *prefork*, and 16 for *event* and *worker*; these limits cannot be raised above 200,000 for *prefork* and 20,000 for *event* and *worker* without recompiling the server.

StartServers S

MPM   5

`StartServers` *number*

Compatibility: event, mpmt_os2, prefork, worker

Number of child server processes created initially on startup.

StartThreads   S

MPM

`StartThreads number`

Compatibility: beos, mpm_netware

Number of threads created at startup. Default is 10 for *beos* and 75 for *mpm_netware*.

ThreadLimit   S

MPM

`ThreadLimit number`

Compatibility: mpm_winnt, worker

Upper limit on configurable number of threads. Default is 1,920 for *mpm_winnt* and 64 for *worker*; these limits cannot be raised above 15,000 for *mpm_winnt* and 20,000 for *worker* without recompiling the server.

ThreadsPerChild   S

MPM   50

`ThreadsPerChild number`

Compatibility: mpm_winnt, worker

Number of threads started by threaded versions of Apache, such as on Windows, which limits the maximum number of connections that can be simultaneously processed.

ThreadStackSize   S

MPM   varies depending on platform

`ThreadStackSize number`

Compatibility: event, mpm_netware, mpm_winnt, worker

Sets the size of the stack for threads that handle client connections and call modules to help process those connections. This can be adjusted upward if Apache crashes due to thread stack overflow, or downward to allow for a greater number of threads.

General Configuration Directives

Optional Features

EnableExceptionHook S

core OFF

`EnableExceptionHook { ON | OFF }`

Compatibility: prefork, worker in 2.0.49 and later

Enables a hook that allows an external module to take action when a child crashes. This directive is only available if Apache has been configured with `--enable-exception-hook`.

EnableMMAP SVDH (FileInfo)

core ON

`EnableMMAP { ON | OFF }`

Controls whether the operating system's memory-mapping features are used to speed up delivery.

Options SVDH (Options)

core All

`Options [+|-]feature ...`

Controls the advanced features that are enabled in a particular context. The options defined in the most restricted context are taken in their entirety unless all features are prefixed with a plus or minus symbol, in which case, those features prefixed with a plus are enabled, those with a minus are disabled, and the remaining features are inherited from the next context out.

`None`
> No extra features are enabled.

`All`
> All options except `MultiViews` are enabled.

`ExecCGI`
> Execution of CGI scripts.

FollowSymLinks
> Controls whether Apache will follow symbolic links (ignored within a `<Location>` section).

Includes
> Server-Side Includes (SSI).

IncludesNOEXEC
> Disables the `#exec` SSI command, as well as the use of `#include` with filenames that refer to CGI scripts.

Indexes
> Controls whether directory listings are generated for URLs that map to directories where there is no directory index file.

MultiViews
> Content-negotiated MultiViews.

SymLinksIfOwnerMatch
> Follows symbolic links only if the owner of the target matches the owner of the link (ignored within `<Location>`).

User and Group

The User and Group directives set the user and group under which Apache processes requests. Resources to be served by Apache must be accessible to this user and group, but it is recommended that system resources are not readable, and certainly not writable, by the user.

User	S
MPM	#-1

`User { `*`username`*` | #`*`uid`*` }`

Compatibility: beos, mpmt_os2, prefork, worker

Username or user ID to which Apache changes while processing requests (the directive is present for compatibility reasons in the *beos* and *mpmt_os2* MPMs but has no effect).

Group   S
MPM   #-1

Group { *group-name* | *#gid* }

Compatibility: beos, mpmt_os2, prefork, worker

Group name or group ID to which Apache changes while processing requests (the directive is present for compatiblity reasons in the *beos* and *mpmt_os2* MPMs but has no effect).

Administrative Files

Depending on the operating system, Apache uses a number of files for communication between the server processes and with utility programs. To reduce security risks, these files should not be located in directories that are world-writable or writable by the user or group specified with the User and Group directives.

CoreDumpDirectory   S
MPM   server root directory

CoreDumpDirectory *directory*

Compatibility: beos, event, mpm_winnt, prefork, worker

Directory in which Apache will dump core in case of a fatal error. The default directory should not be writable by the user specified with the User directive, so no core file will normally be written. Note that core dumps of SSL servers may contain private keys.

LockFile   S
MPM   logs/accept.lock

LockFile *filename*

Compatibility: event, prefork, worker

Lock file used for serializing access to incoming requests. The process ID of the parent process is appended to the name. The path should be changed if the default location is not on a local disk.

PidFile

	S
MPM	logs/httpd.pid

PidFile *filename*

Compatibility: beos, event, mpm_winnt, mpmt_os2, prefork, worker

File in which the process ID of the main server process is recorded. The apachectl utility relies on the PID file being in the standard location.

ScoreBoardFile

	S
MPM	logs/apache_status

ScoreBoardFile *filename*

Compatibility: beos, event, mpm_winnt, prefork, worker

File used for communicating status information between the parent and child server processes. Used only on systems that do not support shared memory.

Loading Shared Objects

Modules may be either compiled into Apache or compiled separately as Dynamic Shared Objects (DSOs)—that is, shared object files on Unix and DLL files on Windows. The following directives are used to load these files and other shared libraries that may be required.

LoadFile

S*

mod_so (B)

LoadFile *filename* ...

Loads the named object or library files, which may contain code required by modules.

LoadModule

S*

mod_so (B)

LoadModule *module filename*

Loads the named DSO module by linking in the object file or library and adding the module structure to the list of active modules.

Request Limits

Request limits are a defense against denial-of-service attacks. If a request exceeds any of the limits, the server returns an error response rather than attempting to service the request.

LimitInternalRecursion

SV

core   10 for both limits

`LimitInternalRecursion number number ...`

Compatibility: 2.0.47 and later

Prevents the server from crashing if it enters an infinite loop of internal redirects or subrequests. The first number is the maximum number of consecutive internal redirects; the second number specifies how deeply subrequests may be nested. If one number is given, it will be used for both limits.

LimitRequestBody

SVDH

core   0

`LimitRequestBody nbytes`

Maximum length of request body that will be accepted. A value of zero means there is no limit.

LimitRequestFields

S

core   100

`LimitRequestFields number`

Limits the number of request header fields that will be accepted.

LimitRequestFieldSize

S

core   8,190

`LimitRequestFieldSize nbytes`

Limits the length of individual request header fields that will be accepted.

LimitRequestLine   S

core   8,190

`LimitRequestLine nbytes`

Maximum length of the request line that will be accepted.

LimitXMLRequestBody   SVDH*

core   1,000,000

`LimitXMLRequestBody bytes`

Specifies the maximum size in bytes of an XML-based request body.
A value of zero disables the limit.

Subprocess Resource Limits

These apply to processes forked by the child server processes,
not to the server processes themselves or to processes forked
by the parent server, such as piped logs.

RLimitCPU   SVDH

core   operating system defaults

`RLimitCPU { secs | max } [secs | max ]`

Soft and hard CPU resource limits, expressed in seconds per process, for processes forked by Apache (including CGI programs).

RLimitMEM   SVDH

core   operating system defaults

`RLimitMEM { bytes | max } [bytes | max ]`

Soft and hard memory resource limits, expressed in bytes per process, for processes forked by Apache.

RLimitNPROC   SVDH

core   operating system defaults

`RLimitNPROC { nprocs | max } [nprocs | max ]`

Soft and hard per-user process limits for processes forked by
Apache. Note that if CGI processes are run under the same user ID

---

as that used by Apache for processing requests, this limit will affect Apache itself.

DBD Framework

The DBD framework module, *mod_dbd*, was introduced in version 2.1 to offer a centralized interface for other modules to use to access SQL databases. *mod_dbd* acts as a frontend to the database API provided by APR. When used with a threaded MPM, it provides connection pooling; for nonthreaded MPMs, it provides persistent connections. In Apache 2.2, *mod_authn_dbd* is the only standard module to use *mod_dbd*, which it uses to retrieve authentication information stored in SQL databases. The corresponding authorization module has not been included in this version, but it is expected to be available in the next version.

DBDExptime   SV

mod_dbd (E)   300 seconds, i.e., 5 minutes

DBDExptime *secs*

Compatibility: threaded MPMs only

Time for which idle connections are kept alive when the maximum number of connections has been exceeded.

DBDKeep   SV

mod_dbd (E)   2

DBDKeep *number*

Compatibility: threaded MPMs only

The base number of connections that should be maintained, even when not in use.

DBDMax   SV

mod_dbd (E)   10

DBDMax *number*

Compatibility: threaded MPMs only

Hard upper limit of connections per process.

DBDMin SV

mod_dbd (E)   1

DBDMin *number*

Compatibility: threaded MPMs only

Minimum number of connections per process.

DBDParams SV*

mod_dbd (E)

DBDParams *string*

Connection string parameters required by the underlying driver.
The interpretation of the string varies from one driver to another:

MySQL

Comma-separated list of *param=value* pairs containing the following information: host, port, dbname, sock, user, pass.

Oracle

Comma-separated list of *param=value* pairs containing the following information: server, dbname, user, pass.

PostgreSQL

Passed straight through to the PostgreSQL client library.

SQLite2

SQLite filename and an integer separated by a comma. The
SQLite2 client library ignores the integer.

SQLite3

Passed straight through to the SQLite3 client library.

DBDPersist SV

mod_dbd (E)   ON

DBDPersist { ON | OFF }

If set to OFF, persistent and pooled connections are disabled and
connections are closed when the query is completed. This is pri-
marily useful for debugging.

DBDPrepareSQL — SV*

mod_dbd (E)

DBDPrepareSQL "statement" label

Prepares a statement at startup and gives it a label. This gives optimum performance for frequently used SQL statements.

DBDriver — SV

mod_dbd (E)

DBDriver name

Selects an APR database driver.

LDAP Framework

The LDAP framework was introduced in version 2.0.41 to offer a centralized interface for other modules to access LDAP servers, acting as a front end to the LDAP API provided by APR. It provides connection pooling and result caching. The *mod_authnz_ldap* authentication and authorization module use it.

LDAPCacheEntries — S

mod_ldap (E) — 1,024

LDAPCacheEntries number

Specifies the maximum number of successful search/bind results that will be cached. If set to zero, caching will be disabled.

LDAPCacheTTL — S

mod_ldap (E) — 600 seconds, i.e., 10 minutes

LDAPCacheTTL secs

Specifies the length of time for which search results are cached.

LDAPConnectionTimeout   S

mod_ldap (E)   10 seconds

`LDAPConnectionTimeout secs`

Timeout value in seconds for the module to attempt to connect to the LDAP server. If the connection is not successful within this period, the module will attempt to connect to a secondary LDAP server, if specified; otherwise, an error will be returned.

LDAPOpCacheEntries   S

mod_ldap (E)   1,024

`LDAPOpCacheEntries number`

The number of cache entries for LDAP compare operations; a value of zero disables operation caching.

LDAPOpCacheTTL   S

mod_ldap (E)   600 seconds, i.e., 10 minutes

`LDAPOpCacheTTL secs`

Time in seconds that entries in the operation cache remain valid.

LDAPSharedCacheFile   S

mod_ldap (E)

`LDAPSharedCacheFile filename`

Full pathname of the shared memory cache file. If not set, anonymous shared memory will be used if the platform supports it.

LDAPSharedCacheSize   S

mod_ldap (E)   102,400 bytes

`LDAPSharedCacheSize nbytes`

Size of the shared memory cache; if set to zero, shared memory caching will not be used.

LDAPTrustedClientCert

mod_ldap (E)

```
LDAPTrustedClientCert type { directory | filename | nickname }
[password]
```

Directory path, filename, or nickname of a per-connection client certificate used when establishing an SSL or TLS connection to an LDAP server. *type* specifies the type of certificate and may be one of the values listed in Table 2-2.

Table 2-2. LDAP certificate types

Type	Description
CERT_BASE64	PEM-encoded client certificate
CERT_DER	Binary DER-encoded client certificate
CERT_NICKNAME	Binary DER-encoded client certificate
KEY_DER	Binary DER-encoded private key
KEY_BASE64	PEM-encoded private key

LDAPTrustedGlobalCert

mod_ldap (E)

```
LDAPTrustedGlobalCert type filename [password]
```

Directory path or filename of the trusted CA certificates and/or system-wide client certificates *mod_ldap* should use when establishing an SSL or TLS connection to an LDAP server. *type* specifies the kind of certificate. Supported types are listed in Table 2-3; they depend on the LDAP toolkit being used.

Table 2-3. LDAP global certificate types

Type	Description
CA_BASE64	PEM-encoded CA certificate
CA_DER	Binary DER-encoded CA certificate
CA_CERT7_DB	Netscape cert7.db CA certificate database file
CA_SECMOD	Netscape secmod database file
CERT_BASE64	PEM-encoded client certificate
CERT_DER	Binary DER-encoded client certificate

Type	Description
CERT_KEY3_DB	Netscape key3.db client certificate database file
CERT_NICKNAME	Binary DER-encoded client certificate
CERT_PFX	PKCS#12-encoded client certificate (Novell SDK)
KEY_DER	Binary DER-encoded private key
KEY_BASE64	PEM-encoded private key
KEY_PFX	PKCS#12-encoded private key (Novell SDK)

LDAPTrustedMode   SV
mod_ldap (E)   None

LDAPTrustedMode *mode*

Specifies the level of encryption required on the connection to the LDAP server.

NONE

> No encryption required

SSL

> Uses an **ldaps** connection on the default port 636

TLS

> Uses **STARTTLS** encryption on an **ldap** connection on the default port 389

If the LDAP server URL specified by the client module uses the **ldaps** scheme, then the mode is always SSL, and the value set by this directive is ignored.

If the underlying LDAP toolkit does not support the mode specified, then connections to the LDAP server will fail.

LDAPVerifyServerCert   S
mod_ldap (E)   ON

LDAPVerifyServerCert { ON | OFF }

Set to ON to force verification of the LDAP server's certificate when establishing an SSL connection to the server.

CHAPTER 3

URL Mapping

URL mapping, or translation, is the first major stage in request handling. Later stages, such as access controls and content type determination, work with the translated URL.

Initial Environment Setup

The *mod_setenvif* module is run before URL translation for main and virtual server contexts and after URL translation for directory sections and *.htaccess* files. At this point, only the values of the request line and of the HTTP request headers are available. *mod_setenvif* sets environment variables based on these values; the variables are in turn often used to control URL rewriting, authentication, conditional logging, and other conditional behaviors.

There are a number of special environment variables that, if set, modify the response of the server, particularly to cope with buggy clients. *mod_proxy* defines further special variables related to proxying; these are covered in Chapter 9.

downgrade-1.0

> Forces the request to be treated as an HTTP/1.0 request

force-gzip

> Forces output compression if the DEFLATE filter is activated

`force-no-vary`

> Forces any **Vary** headers to be removed from the response (implies `force-response-1.0`)

`force-response-1.0`

> Forces Apache to respond with an HTTP/1.0 response

`gzip-only-text/html`

> Disables compression for content types other than `text/html` if the value is set to 1

`no-gzip`

> Disables compressed output

`nokeepalive`

> Disables keepalive

`prefer-language`

> Indicates a preferred language that overrides the content negotiation process and takes precedence over the client's preferences

`redirect-carefully`

> Disables redirects on non-`GET` requests for directories that do not include the trailing slash

`suppress-error-charset`

> Forces Apache to omit the character set on redirects

The environment variable **UNIQUE_ID** is set to a globally unique identifier for each request if the *mod_unique_id* module is loaded.

SetEnvIf   SVDH* (FileInfo)

mod_setenvif (B)

SetEnvIf *attribute regex* { !*var* | *var*[=*value*] } ...

Sets an environment variable if the value of the attribute matches the regular expression. The attribute may be an attribute of the request (taken from the following list), a request header field, or an environment variable set with an earlier **SetEnvIf**-type directive.

Remote_Host

> The hostname of the client, if available; otherwise, its IP address

Remote_Addr

The IP address of the client

Server_Addr

The IP address on which the request was received (2.0.43 and later)

Request_Method

The HTTP method used for the request

Request_Protocol

The name and version of the protocol used for the request

Request_URI

The portion of the URL following the scheme and host components

If the variable name is preceded by an exclamation mark (!), the variable will be unset; otherwise, it is set to the value specified or to 1 if no value is specified.

SetEnvIfNoCase   SVDH* (FileInfo)

mod_setenvif (B)

SetEnvIfNoCase *attribute regex* { !*var* | *var*[=*value*] } ...

Identical to the SetEnvIf directive, except that pattern matching is performed case-insensitively.

BrowserMatch   SV*

mod_setenvif (B)

BrowserMatch *regexp* { !*var* | *var*[=*value*] } ...

Special case of the SetEnvIf directive; the attribute tested is the User-Agent HTTP request header.

BrowserMatchNoCase   SV*

mod_setenvif (B)

BrowserMatchNoCase *regexp* { !*var* | *var*[=*value*] } ...

Identical to the BrowserMatch directive, except that pattern matching is performed case-insensitively.

Basic URL Translation

The core only performs a simple mapping from URLs to filenames, by appending the local part of the URL to the document root. Other modules provide more sophisticated mappings.

DocumentRoot   SV

core   depends on compilation settings

`DocumentRoot directory`

Top level directory for web documents. Requests for documents not mapped by other directives are mapped to filenames formed by appending the request path to this directory.

AcceptPathInfo   SVDH (FileInfo)

core   Default

`AcceptPathInfo { ON | OFF | Default }`

Compatibility: 2.0.30 and later

If set to OFF, requests that do not map exactly to existing files will be rejected with a 404 (Not Found) error. If set to ON, requests that map to files, plus additional pathinfo will be accepted. If set to Default, then the response to such requests is determined by the handler responsible for the request.

AllowEncodedSlashes   SV

core   OFF

`AllowEncodedSlashes { ON | OFF }`

Compatibility: 2.0.46 and later

Controls whether URLs containing encoded slashes (%2F for forward slash, and %5C for backslash) are allowed or rejected with a 404 (Not Found) error. Does not control decoding of encoded slashes.

Aliases and Redirects

The *mod_alias* and *mod_userdir* modules provide alternative mappings.

Alias   SV*

mod_alias (B)

`Alias` *url-path-prefix real-path-prefix*

Specifies a mapping from URLs to filenames. If, after URL decoding, the document's URL matches the URL prefix, the prefix is removed and replaced with the real path prefix.

AliasMatch   SV*

mod_alias (B)

`AliasMatch` *url-regex path-replacement*

Specifies a mapping from URLs to filenames using regular expressions. Substrings matched by parenthesized subexpressions can be interpolated into *path-replacement* by specifying the number of the subexpression prefixed by a dollar sign (**$**).

Redirect   SVDH* (FileInfo)

mod_alias (B)

`Redirect` [*status*] *url-path-prefix new-prefix*

Maps matching URLs to new locations, returning a redirection response to the client. *status* may be one of the following:

permanent

> Returns a 301 (Moved Permanently) status, indicating that the resource has been moved permanently

temp

> Returns a 302 (Found) status, indicating that the resource has moved temporarily

seeother

> Returns a 303 (See Other) status, indicating that the resource has been replaced

gone

> Returns a 410 (Gone) status, indicating that the resource has been permanently removed (the *new-prefix* argument should be omitted in this case)

If *status* is not specified, then a temporary redirection response is generated.

RedirectMatch   SVDH* (FileInfo)

mod_alias (**B**)

`RedirectMatch [status] url-regex new-url`

Maps a URL to a new URL using regular expressions. Substrings matched by parenthesized subexpressions can be interpolated into *new-url* by specifying the number of the subexpression prefixed by a dollar sign (**$**).

RedirectPermanent   SVDH* (FileInfo)

mod_alias (**B**)

`RedirectPermanent url-path new-url`

Generates a 301 (Moved Permanently) redirection status for matching URLs.

RedirectTemp   SVDH* (FileInfo)

mod_alias (**B**)

`RedirectTemp url-path new-url`

Generates a 302 (Found) temporary redirection status for matching URLs.

ScriptAlias   SV*

mod_alias (**B**)

`ScriptAlias url-path-prefix script-dir`

Maps *url-path-prefix* to *script-dir* and marks the handler as cgi-script, causing matching URLs to be treated as requests for CGI scripts.

ScriptAliasMatch SV*

mod_alias (B)

ScriptAliasMatch *url-regex script-dir*

Specifies a mapping from URLs to CGI scripts using regular expressions. Substrings matched by parenthesized subexpressions can be interpolated into *script-dir* by specifying the number of the subexpression prefixed by a dollar sign ($).

Requests for Directories

The *mod_dir* module handles requests that map to directories. This is separate from the automatic directory index generation, which is handled by *mod_autoindex*.

DirectoryIndex SVDH* (Indexes)

mod_dir (B) index.html

DirectoryIndex *local-url* ...

Lists resources to look for when a request maps to a directory name. The first one found is used. If none of the resources can be found, *mod_autoindex* is enabled and the Indexes option is set; then a directory listing will be automatically generated.

DirectorySlash SVDH (Indexes)

mod_dir (E) ON

DirectorySlash { ON | OFF }

Compatibility: 2.0.51 and later

If set to ON, then requests which map to a directory but which do not end in a trailing slash will be redirected back to the same URL with a trailing slash appended, enabling automatic directory indexes and relative URLs to work correctly.

URL Rewriting with mod_rewrite

The *mod_rewrite* module is a sophisticated, pattern-based URL rewriting engine that lets you set up complex rewriting rules that specify qualifying conditions, using the RewriteRule and RewriteCond directives. These directives allow submatches, CGI variables, and other information to be interpolated into replacement strings and condition strings as shown in Table 3-1.

Table 3-1. Information that can be interpolated

Construct	Expansion
$n	Back-reference to the nth parenthesized group of the RewriteRule pattern.
%n	Back-reference to the nth parenthesized group part of the last matching RewriteCond pattern.
%{var}	The value of the named CGI variable.
%{ENV:var}	The value of the named environment variable.
%{HTTP:header}	The value of the named HTTP header.
%{LA-F:var}	*File look-ahead*: issues an internal subrequest based on the filename to determine the final value of the named variable.
%{LA-U:var}	*URL look-ahead*: issues an internal subrequest based on the URL to determine the final value of the named variable.
${map:key[|def]}	The value returned by the named map function (only valid in RewriteRule). key is the value to look up, which will normally be an interpolated value. def is the value to use if the lookup fails.

mod_rewrite allows the variables listed in Table 3-2 to be used in RewriteCond and RewriteRule directives, in addition to the standard CGI variables.

Table 3-2. Additional mod_rewrite variables

Variable	Description
TIME	Current date and time
TIME_YEAR	Current year
TIME_MON	Current month

Variable	Description
TIME_DAY	Current day of the month
TIME_HOUR	Hour of the current day
TIME_MIN	Minutes of the current hour
TIME_SEC	Seconds of the current minute
TIME_WDAY	Current day of the week

RewriteBase   DH (FileInfo)

mod_rewrite (E)   the current directory pathname

RewriteBase *url-path*

Base URL for per-directory transformations.

RewriteCond   SVDH* (FileInfo)

mod_rewrite (E)

RewriteCond *string* [!]*condition*   [[*flags*]]

Specifies a condition for the following RewriteRule to match. *string* may contain interpolated sequences. *condition* may be a regular expression or one of the conditions listed in Table 3-3.

Table 3-3. Conditions supported by RewriteCond

Condition	Description
-d	*string* is a directory.
-f	*string* is a regular file.
-s	*string* is a nonempty regular file.
-l	*string* is a symbolic link.
-F	*string* is a valid and accessible file.
-U	*string* is a valid and accessible URL.
=*string2*	*string* is identical to *string2*.
<*string2*	*string* is lexicographically less than *string2*.
>*string2*	*string* is lexicographically greater than *string2*.

A comma-separated list of flags, specified in full or abbreviated as listed in Table 3-4, may be specified as a third argument, enclosed in square brackets.

Table 3-4. RewriteCond flags

Flag	Description
{ NC | nocase }	Compares strings case-insensitively
{ NV | novary }	If the condition uses an HTTP header, does not add the header to the Vary header of the response
{ OR | ornext }	Combines the current condition with the next one using a logical OR (by default, conditions are AND-ed together)

RewriteEngine   SVDH (FileInfo)
mod_rewrite (E)   OFF

RewriteEngine { ON | OFF }

Enables or disables the rewriting engine.

RewriteLock   S
mod_rewrite (E)

RewriteLock *filename*

The lock file to be used for synchronizing access to **prg**-type maps.

RewriteLog   SV
mod_rewrite (E)

RewriteLog { *filename* | "|*command*" }

Name of the log file for the rewriting engine. If the argument starts with a vertical bar character (|), then the rest of the argument is regarded as a command line that was executed and passed rewrite error messages on its standard input.

RewriteLogLevel

SV

mod_rewrite (E)

0

RewriteLogLevel *level*

Controls the verbosity of logging on a scale from zero to nine. Zero disables logging, while levels greater than two may be useful for debugging but can have a severe impact upon performance.

RewriteMap

SV*

mod_rewrite (E)

RewriteMap *map-name map-type:map-source*

Defines a map, which can be used in mapping functions within rule substitution strings. The following map types are supported:

txt:*file*

> *file* is a text file; each line contains a key–value pair separated by whitespace.

rnd:*file*

> *file* is a text file; each line contains a key and a sequence of values separated by a vertical bar (|), one of which will be chosen at random.

dbm:*file*

> *file* is a hashed DBM file.

prg:*program*

> *program* is a program that is started at server startup. It is fed keys as newline-terminated strings on its standard input, and it is expected to output a value for each newline-terminated string on its standard output.

int:*function*

> *function* is one of the following internal functions: toupper, tolower, escape, or unescape.

RewriteOptions

SVDH (FileInfo)

mod_rewrite (E)

`RewriteOptions option`

The only option is inherit, which means that virtual hosts inherit the environment from the main server, and per-directory configuration files inherit it from their parent directory.

RewriteRule

SVDH* (FileInfo)

mod_rewrite (E)

`RewriteRule [!]pattern replacement [[flags]]`

Compares the current URL with the regular expression *pattern* and substitutes *replacement*, interpolating any marked constructs, if the pattern matches (or does not match if preceded by "!") and any preceding conditions are met.

The replacement may be specified as "-", in which case, no substitution is performed, but any chained rules are evaluated.

A comma-separated list of flags, specified in full or abbreviated as listed in Table 3-5, may be specified as a third argument, enclosed in square brackets.

Table 3-5. RewriteRule flags

Flag	Description
{ C | chain }	Chains current rule with the next rule
{ E | env }=*var*:*val*	Sets environment variable
{ F | forbidden }	Terminates with 403 (Forbidden) status
{ G | gone }	Returns 410 (Gone) status
{ L | last }	Stops applying rewriting rules
{ N | next }	Starts applying rules from the top against the current URL
{ NC | nocase }	Matches case-insensitively
{ NS | nosubreq }	Skips the rule if processing an internal subrequest
{ P | proxy }	Passes the request off to *mod_proxy*
{ PT | passthrough }	Passes the result through to the next handler

Flag	Description
{ QSA | qsappend }	Appends to existing query string
{ R | redirect }[=*code*]	Forces a redirect
{ S | skip }=*n*	Skips *n* rules
{ T | type }=*type*	Sets the MIME type to *type*

Content Negotiated Documents

Content negotiation allows the best variant of a resource that is available in multiple representations to be selected according to the values of the Accept-type HTTP request headers. The available variants may be determined automatically if the requested resource does not exist and the MultiViews option is enabled for the directory. Alternatively, variants and their attributes may be specified explicitly in a type map file, if the requested URI is for the type map file and the handler is set to type-map.

A type map file contains a number of stanzas comprising header records (such as Content-Type and Content-Encoding) that define the attributes for a variant. The URI header gives the path of the variant relative to the map file.

CacheNegotiatedDocs   SV

mod_negotiation (B)   OFF

CacheNegotiatedDocs { ON | OFF }

Allows content-negotiated documents to be cached by proxies. Applies only to HTTP/1.0 requests.

LanguagePriority   SVDH (FileInfo)

mod_negotiation (B)

LanguagePriority *MIME-language* ...

Sets the precedence in decreasing order for language variants when a document is selected by MultiViews and the client does not specify a preference with the HTTP Accept-Language header.

ForceLanguagePriority

SVDH (FileInfo)

mod_negotiation (B) Prefer

ForceLanguagePriority { None | Prefer | Fallback } [Prefer | Fallback]

Compatibility: 2.0.30 and later

Controls how the language selection process is resolved. If Prefer is specified and the browser specifies multiple acceptable and available languages with equal preference, then the first language listed with LanguagePriority is used. If Fallback is specified and no acceptable languages are available, then the first language listed with LanguagePriority is used.

User Directories

The *mod_userdir* module allows individual users to have their own web directories, identified by URL paths starting with *~username*.

UserDir

SV*

mod_userdir (B) public_html

UserDir { *directory* | DISABLED [*user* ...] | ENABLED *user* ... }

Specifies how requests for user-specific documents (with URL paths starting *~username*) are handled. This directive performs a number of different functions according to the value of its first argument:

Keyword DISABLED *without any usernames*
> Username-directory translation is disabled except for those usernames explicitly enabled.

Keyword DISABLED *followed by a list of usernames*
> Usernames listed are not translated, even if they appear in a UserDir ENABLED directive.

Keyword ENABLED *followed by a list of usernames*
> Usernames listed will be translated unless they are explicitly disabled.

Relative directory name
> URL path after *~username* will be mapped to the named sub-directory within the user's home directory.

Absolute pathname or URL containing an asterisk (*)
> The asterisk will be replaced with the username, or, if there is no asterisk, the username will be appended to the path. The part of the URL after *~username* will be appended to the path.

Correcting Misspelled URLs

The *mod_speling* [sic] module attempts to satisfy requests for nonexistent files by checking to see whether similar files exist that differ in case or by one character; if more than one file matches, the client is sent a list of matches. Note that enabling this module can have an adverse performance impact, and more seriously could also cause unintended files to be served.

CheckCaseOnly   SVDH (Options)

mod_speling (E)	OFF

`CheckCaseOnly { ON | OFF }`

Limits *mod_speling* to matching files that differ only in the case of the individual letters.

CheckSpelling   SVDH (Options)

mod_speling (E)	OFF

`CheckSpelling { ON | OFF }`

Enables URLs that translate to nonexistent files to match existing files where the filenames differ in capitalization and may contain a single insertion, deletion, transposition, or wrong character.

Imagemaps

Imagemaps define mappings from regions of an image in an HTML document to URLs or other actions (the image element must be marked with the `ismap` attribute for it to be treated as an imagemap). Client-side imagemaps are handled entirely by the web browser. However, server-side imagemaps cause the browser to issue a GET request for the URL specified in the enclosing HTML `<a>` element, with the *x* and *y* coordinates of the point clicked passed as the query string value. Server-side imagemaps are not used often nowadays, probably because client-side imagemaps are more powerful, and they are well supported in web page editing tools.

Server-side imagemaps are set up by associating a handler of `imap-file` with a map file that contains comments (denoted by a leading "#"), blank lines, and directives, as listed below:

base *url*
> Base URL for relative URLs in the map file (overrides the `ImapBase` directive).

default *action* ["*text*"]
> Action to take if the coordinates do not fall within any of the defined regions and there are no defined points. Defaults to `nocontent`.

circle *action* ["*text*"] *x1,y1 x2,y2* ["*text*"]
> Defines a circular region specified by the coordinates of the center and a point on the circumference.

point *action* ["*text*"] *x,y* ["*text*"]
> Defines a point specified by the coordinate pair. If the selected point falls outside any of the areas defined with `circle`, `poly`, and `rect` directives, then the closest point is taken.

poly *action* ["*text*"] *x1,y1 x2,y2 x3,y3* ... ["*text*"]
> Defines a polygonal region specified by the coordinates of the vertices. Between 3 and 100 vertices may be specified.

rect *action* ["*text*"] *x1,y1 x2,y2* ["*text*"]
> Defines a rectangular region specified by the coordinates of two opposing corners.

The quoted `text` is used as the text of the link if a menu is generated. It may appear before or after the coordinates.

The actions may be one of those listed in Table 3-6.

Table 3-6. Imagemap actions

Action	Description
url	Destination URL of the link—either absolute or relative to the base value
map	Generates an HTML index unless ImapMenu is set to None
menu	Synonymous with map
referer	Equivalent to the URL of the referring document or to the URL of the server if the request did not contain a Referer header
nocontent	Sends a response with status 204 (No Content) that tells the client to continue to display the same page (not valid for base)
error	Sends an error response with status 500 (Internal Server Error)

ImapBase
SVDH (Indexes)

mod_imagemap (B)

ImapBase { map | referer | *url* }

Base URL for the imagemap. The default uses the current scheme (http, https, ftp, etc.) on the current server. May be overridden by a base directive in the map file.

ImapDefault
SVDH (Indexes)

mod_imagemap (B)   nocontent

ImapDefault { error | nocontent | referer | menu | *url* }

The default action for the imagemap. May be overridden by a default directive in the map file.

ImapMenu
SVDH (Indexes)

mod_imagemap (B)   formatted

ImapMenu { none | formatted | semiformatted | unformatted }

Controls whether a menu document is generated if the request for an imagemap file does not contain valid coordinates.

> No menu is generated, and the default action is performed as specified by the ImapDefault Apache directive or the default map file directive.

`formatted`
> A simple menu document is generated from the map file—consisting of a heading and a list of links—and returned.

`semiformatted`
> A menu document is generated from the map file using the contents of the comments and HTML breaks in place of blank lines.

`unformatted`
> A menu document is generated from the map file using the contents of the comments but ignoring blank lines.

Mass Virtual Hosting

The *mod_vhost_alias* module allows the document root and CGI script directories for all matching virtual hosts to be specified as templates, into which parts of the hostname or IP address are interpolated, as indicated by the specifiers listed in Table 3-7.

Table 3-7. Vhost directory template specifiers

Spec	Description
%p	Replaced with the port number of the virtual host.
%n	Replaced with the *n*th dot-separated component of the hostname or IP address. If *n* is zero, then the whole string is used. If *n* is preceded by a minus sign, then it counts from the end of the hostname or IP address. If the specifier is suffixed by a plus sign, then the rest of the hostname or IP address is used.
%n.m	Replaced with the *m*th character of what would be selected by %n.
%%	Replaced with a single percent sign (%).

VirtualDocumentRoot   SV

mod_vhost_alias (E)

`VirtualDocumentRoot` *directory-template*

URLs for a matching virtual host are translated to filenames by prepending a document root directory formed by interpolating the value of the server name into *directory-template*.

VirtualDocumentRootIP

mod_vhost_alias (E)

VirtualDocumentRootIP *directory-template*

Identical to VirtualDocumentRoot, except the IP address is used rather than the server name.

VirtualScriptAlias

mod_vhost_alias (E)

VirtualScriptAlias *directory-template*

URLs for a matching virtual host that start with /cgi-bin/ are translated to filenames by prepending a script directory formed by interpolating the value of the server name into *directory-template*. The handler is marked as cgi-script so that the file will be processed as such.

VirtualScriptAliasIP

mod_vhost_alias (E)

VirtualScriptAliasIP *directory-template*

Identical to VirtualScriptAlias, except the IP address is used rather than the server name.

CHAPTER 4

Access Controls

Access to resources can be restricted by authorization rules based on an authenticated user and by non-user-based access controls. If non-user-based access controls are specified, they are applied first. Authentication is only performed if needed to evaluate authorization rules specified with Require directives. Access controls and authorization rules can be restricted to particular HTTP methods by enclosing them in <Limit> or <LimitExcept> blocks.

Access controls can also be implemented with *mod_rewrite*, and the *mod_ssl* module provides SSL-based access control features.

Non-User-Based Access Controls

The *mod_authz_host* module implements non-user-based access controls. These are usually host-based but can also be tied to environment variables. Hosts are specified by full or partial domain names, full or partial IP addresses, network/ netmask pairs, or network/prefix-length pairs.

If authorization rules and non-user-based access controls are specified, the Satisfy directive determines whether requests have to satisfy either or both; authentication and authorization will be skipped if, having evaluated the access controls,

Apache can determine definitively whether access is allowed or denied.

Allow
DH* (Limit)

mod_authz_host (B)

`Allow from  { all | { host | env=var } ... }`

Allows requests to a resource from the specified hosts or with the specified environment variable set.

Deny
DH* (Limit)

mod_authz_host (B)

`Deny from  { all | { host | env=var } ... }`

Denies requests to a resource from the specified hosts or with the specified environment variable set.

Order
DH (Limit)
deny,allow

mod_authz_host (B)

`Order { allow,deny | deny,allow | mutual-failure }`

Specifies the order in which Allow and Deny directives are evaluated.

allow,deny
> Allow directives are applied before Deny directives. Any unmatched requests are denied.

deny,allow
> Deny directives are applied before Allow directives. Any unmatched requests are allowed.

mutual-failure
> Only requests that match an Allow directive and are not forbidden by a Deny directive are allowed.

Satisfy
DH (AuthConfig)
All

core

`Satisfy { All | Any }`

Policy applied if both authorization rules and non-user-based access controls are specified for a resource. All means that both sets of rules must be satisfied, whereas Any means that only one or the other needs to be satisfied, which can be used to allow nonauthenticated access from machines on a secure network while requiring accesses from other hosts to be authenticated.

Authentication

Authentication is the process of verifying that the client credentials required for authorization are valid. Authentication is skipped if no authorization is specified.

Authentication Setup

There are two schemes specified for HTTP authentication in RFC 2617: Basic and Digest. As of Apache 2.1, the handling of each scheme is implemented in a separate module, selected with the AuthType directive. Both schemes use realms to differentiate between protection spaces, and this is set with AuthName.

The mechanism for storing user credentials is delegated to authentication provider modules, selected with either AuthBasicProvider or AuthDigestProvider.

AuthDefaultAuthoritative   DH (AuthConfig)

mod_authn_default (B)   ON

AuthDefaultAuthoritative { ON | OFF }

mod_authn_default is an authentication fallback module that just rejects all credentials. If this directive is set to OFF, authentication will be passed to other modules; this may be useful in conjunction with third-party modules.

AuthName   DH (AuthConfig)

core

AuthName *realm-name*

Authentication realm for documents matched by the enclosing section. A realm identifies a set of resources residing on the same server

---

and protected by the same set of passwords. Note that Apache does not prevent different, inconsistent authentication databases from being used within the same realm, which can lead to unpredictable results.

AuthType   DH (AuthConfig)

core

AuthType { Basic | Digest }

The authentication scheme to use.

HTTP Basic Authentication

The *mod_auth_basic* module implements HTTP Basic authentication. This scheme passes usernames and passwords across the network without encryption and cannot be not considered a secure method of authentication unless used in conjunction with SSL/TLS.

AuthBasicAuthoritative   DH (AuthConfig)
mod_auth_basic (E)   ON

AuthBasicAuthoritative { ON | OFF }

Normally, if none of the provider modules indicates successful authentication, *mod_auth_basic* will deny access with a 401 (Unauthorized) response. If this directive is set to OFF, authentication will fall back to other non-provider-based modules; this should only be necessary with third-party modules.

AuthBasicProvider   DH (AuthConfig)
mod_auth_basic (E)   file

AuthBasicProvider *provider* ...

Specifies the provider modules to be used to authenticate users when using Basic authentication; each module is called in turn until one indicates successful authentication or the list is exhausted. The modules, specified using the identifiers listed in Table 4-1, must be present in the server.

HTTP Digest Authentication

The *mod_auth_digest* module implements HTTP Digest authentication. Digest authentication addresses the serious security flaws in Basic authentication. Browser support for the scheme was once an issue, but that is less the case now; and although it is still marked as experimental, it is currently used in production environments.

AuthDigestAlgorithm

DH (AuthConfig)

mod_auth_digest (X)   MD5

```
AuthDigestAlgorithm { MD5 | MD5-sess }
```

Specifies the digest algorithm to be used. As of version 2.2.9, only the MD5 algorithm is working.

AuthDigestDomain

DH* (AuthConfig)

mod_auth_digest (X)

```
AuthDigestDomain uri ...
```

Specifies one or more URIs that are in the same protection space, i.e., that share the same realm, usernames, and passwords.

AuthDigestNcCheck

S

mod_auth_digest (X)   OFF

```
AuthDigestNcCheck { ON | OFF }
```

Documented as controlling whether checking of the server-generated nonce count is enabled; but as of version 2.2.9, the directive does nothing.

AuthDigestNonceFormat

DH (AuthConfig)

mod_auth_digest (X)

```
AuthDigestNonceFormat format
```

Documented as specifying the format of generated nonces; but as of version 2.2.9, the directive does nothing.

AuthDigestNonceLifetime

DH (AuthConfig)

mod_auth_digest (X)   300 seconds, i.e., 5 minutes

`AuthDigestNonceLifetime secs`

Specifies how long the server nonce is valid.

AuthDigestProvider

DH (AuthConfig)

mod_auth_digest (X)   file

`AuthDigestProvider provider ...`

Specifies the provider module to be used to authenticate users when using Digest authentication (see Table 4-1).

AuthDigestQop

DH* (AuthConfig)

mod_auth_digest (X)   auth

`AuthDigestQop { none | auth | auth-int } [auth | auth-int ] ...`

Specifies the *quality of protection* options to be used. `auth` provides authentication checking of username and password; `auth-int` provides authentication and integrity checking (but is not implemented as of version 2.2.9); `none` causes Apache to use the older RFC2069 standard, which does not include quality of protection options in the server response.

AuthDigestShmemSize

DH (AuthConfig)

mod_auth_digest (X)   1,000

`AuthDigestShmemSize nbytes`

The amount of shared memory to use to keep track of clients. *nbytes* may be suffixed with the letters `K` or `M` to specify values in kilobytes or megabytes respectively.

Authentication Providers

Authentication provider modules are responsible for managing authentication credentials using flat files, databases, or other storage mechanisms. The standard authentication providers are listed in Table 4-1.

Table 4-1. Authentication provider identifiers

Identifier	Authentication source
anon	Anonymous authentication (*mod_authn_dbm*)
dbd	Relational database (*mod_authn_dbd*)
dbm	Embedded database file (*mod_authn_dbm*)
file	Plain text file (*mod_authn_file*)
ldap	LDAP server (*mod_authnz_ldap*)
user defined	Extended provider (*mod_authn_alias*)

Credentials Stored in Plain Text Files

Authentication against plain text password files is supported
by the *mod_authn_file* provider module, which is identified as
file. It is the default provider. This is the simplest mechanism
to set up; however, searching through text files is inefficient for
large numbers of users.

Password files used for Basic authentication files can be
managed with the htpasswd utility. MD5, crypt(), and SHA
password encryption methods are supported. For Digest
authentication, the htdigest utility is used to manage password
files.

AuthUserFile   DH (AuthConfig)

mod_authn_file (B)

AuthUserFile *filename*

The path to the plain text password file.

Credentials Stored in DBM Files

The *mod_auth_dbm* module is an authentication provider, identified as **dbd**, that supports storage of user credentials in DBM files. Depending on how it is built, a number of different DBM formats are supported. The files can be managed with the **dbmmanage** utility. The files can include group membership and encrypted passwords, so they can be used for authorization as well as authentication.

AuthDBMType   DH
mod_authn_dbm (E)   `default`

`AuthDBMType { default | SDBM | GDBM | NDBM | DB }`

Indicates the database file format for the user DBM file. The available formats are determined at compile time, as is the default type.

AuthDBMUserFile   DH (`AuthConfig`)
mod_authn_dbm (E)

`AuthDBMUserFile filename`

The path to the DBM file containing usernames and passwords for authentication.

Credentials Stored in a Relational Database

The *mod_auth_dbd* module is an authentication provider, identified as **dbd**, that allows usernames and passwords to be stored in a relational database. It relies on the *mod_dbd* module to access the underlying database.

AuthDBDUserPWQuery

D (AuthConfig)

mod_authn_dbd (E)

`AuthDBDUserPWQuery` *query*

The SQL query that is run to look up the password for a user. The query string should include the specifier %s, which will be replaced with the user's ID.

AuthDBDUserRealmQuery

D (AuthConfig)

mod_authn_dbd (E)

`AuthDBDUserRealmQuery` *query*

The SQL query to be run to look up a user's password. The user's ID and realm are denoted in the query, in that order, by %s specifiers.

Anonymous Authentication

The *mod_auth_anon* module is an authentication provider, identified as anon, that allows anonymous authentication in a manner similar to anonymous FTP.

Anonymous

DH* (AuthConfig)

mod_authn_anon (E)

`Anonymous` *username* ...

List of *magic usernames* that are allowed access without password verification. Note that the usernames are case-insensitive and, if enclosed in double or single quotes, may include spaces.

Anonymous_LogEmail

DH (AuthConfig)

ON

mod_authn_anon (E)

`Anonymous_LogEmail { ON | OFF }`

If set to ON, the client's password is logged to the error log.

Anonymous_MustGiveEmail

DH (AuthConfig)

ON

mod_authn_anon (E)

`Anonymous_MustGiveEmail { ON | OFF }`

If set to ON, the client must supply a nonblank password.

Anonymous_NoUserId

DH (AuthConfig)

mod_authn_anon (E)

OFF

`Anonymous_NoUserId { ON | OFF }`

If set to ON, an empty username is acceptable.

Anonymous_VerifyEmail

DH (AuthConfig)

mod_authn_anon (E)

OFF

`Anonymous_VerifyEmail { ON | OFF }`

If set to ON, the password is checked to ensure it contains an at sign (@) and a period (.), that is, that it looks at least vaguely like an email address.

Extended Authentication Providers

The *mod_authn_alias* allows extended authentication providers to be defined. These can then be referenced in multiple locations.

<AuthnProviderAlias>

S* (AuthConfig)

mod_authn_alias (E)

`<AuthnProviderAlias base-provider alias >`
`    ...`
`</AuthnProviderAlias>`

Compatibility: 2.1 and later

Defines *alias* as an extended authentication provider based on a base provider, with settings specified by the authentication directives enclosed in the container.

Authorization

Authorization is the process of verifying that an authenticated user is permitted to access a particular resource.

Authorization Setup

Each authorization rule is specified with a `Require` directive. The rules themselves are implemented by individual authorization modules.

AuthzDefaultAuthoritative DH (AuthConfig)

mod_authz_default (E) ON

`AuthzDefaultAuthoritative { ON | OFF }`

mod_authn_default is an authorization fallback module that just rejects any authorization request. If this directive is set to `OFF`, authorization will be passed to other modules; this may be useful in conjunction with third-party modules.

Require DH* (AuthConfig)

core

`Require requirement [arg ...]`

Authorization requirement for an authenticated user to be allowed access to a resource. The requirements implemented by standard authorization modules are as follows, with the modules implementing the requirement in parentheses:

file-group *filename*
> The authenticated username must be a member of an authorization group that matches the name of the system group that owns the specified file (*mod_authz_owner*, and *mod_authz_dbm* or *mod_authz_groupfile*).

file-owner *filename*
> The authenticated username must match the name of the system user that owns the specified file (*mod_authz_owner*).

group *group* ...
> The authenticated username must be a member of one of the specified authorization groups (*mod_authz_groupfile* or *mod_authz_dbm*).

user *user* ...
> The authenticated user must be one of the specified users (*mod_authz_user*).

```
valid-user
```
All authenticated users are authorized (*mod_authz_user*).

Explicit User Authorization

The *mod_authz_user* module implements two authorization rules: **user** to check the authenticated username against a specified list of usernames, and **valid-user** to treat all authenticated users as authorized.

AuthzUserAuthoritative | DH (AuthConfig)

mod_authz_user (E) | ON

```
AuthzUserAuthoritative { ON | OFF }
```

Specifies whether the *mod_authz_user* module is authoritative for authorization, or should fall back to other modules on failure.

Group Membership Stored in Plain Text Files

The *mod_authz_groupfile* module implements the **group** authorization rule, which checks the authenticated username against a list of groups stored in a plain text file. Each line consists of a group name followed by a colon and a space-separated list of the usernames of the members of the group. The module also provides support for the **file-group** rule.

AuthGroupFile | DH (AuthConfig)

mod_authz_groupfile (B)

```
AuthGroupFile filename
```

The name of the plain text file defining group membership.

AuthzGroupFileAuthoritative | DH (AuthConfig)

mod_authz_groupfile (E) | ON

```
AuthzGroupFileAuthoritative { ON | OFF }
```

Specifies whether the *mod_authz_groupfile* module is authoritative for authorization or should fall back to other modules on failure.

Group Membership Stored in DBM Files

The *mod_authz_dbm* module implements the `group` authorization rule, which checks the authenticated username against a DBM file. The key is the username, and the value contains a comma-separated list of groups to which the user belongs. Group membership may be stored in the user file by setting the group DBM file to be the same as the user DBM file, and by storing a comma-separated list of groups in the value for each user, separated from the password by a colon. The module also provides support for the `file-group` rule.

AuthDBMGroupFile   DH (AuthConfig)
mod_authz_dbm (E)

`AuthDBMGroupFile filename`

The path to the DBM file containing group membership lists for authentication.

AuthzDBMAuthoritative   DH (AuthConfig)
mod_authz_dbm (E)   ON

`AuthzDBMAuthoritative { ON | OFF }`

Specifies whether the *mod_authz_dbm* module is authoritative for authorization or should fall back to other modules on failure.

AuthzDBMType   SVDH* (AuthConfig)
mod_authz_dbm (E)   default

`AuthzDBMType { default | SDBM | GDBM | NDBM | DB }`

Specifies the database file format used for the group DBM file. The available formats are determined at compile time, as is the default type.

Authorization Based on File Ownership

The *mod_authz_owner* module implements the `file-owner` authorization rule, which checks the authenticated username against the name of the system owner who owns the file, and the `file-group` rule, which checks that the username is a member of the group owning the file. The latter rule requires a group authorization module.

AuthzOwnerAuthoritative _____ DH (AuthConfig)

mod_authz_owner (E)   ON

`AuthzOwnerAuthoritative { ON | OFF }`

Specifies whether the *mod_authz_owner* module is authoritative for authorization or should fall back to other modules on failure.

LDAP Authentication and Authorization

The *mod_authz_ldap* module is both an authentication provider, named `ldap`, and an authorization module that authenticates against an LDAP server. It relies on the services of the *mod_ldap* module to access LDAP servers.

The module adds a number of authorization rules to the `Require` directive:

`ldap-attribute` *attribute=value* ...
> The attributes of the user must match any of the attributes specified.

`ldap-dn` *distinguished-name*
> The DN found in the search phase must match the specified value. Note that everything after `ldap-group` is regarded as a single argument and does not require quoting.

`ldap-filter` *filter*
> The DN returned by the filter search must match the DN of the authenticated user.

`ldap-group` *group-dn*
> The user must be a member of the specified LDAP group. Note that everything after `ldap-group` is regarded as a single argument and does not require quoting.

`ldap-user` *user* ...
> Space-separated list of usernames. If the names contain spaces, they must be enclosed in quotes.

Other Require rules, such as valid-user, may be used with
LDAP authentication. The appropriate authorization module
must be present in the server, and AuthzLDAPAuthoritative
must be set to OFF.

LDAP Configuration Directives

AuthLDAPCharsetConfig   S (AuthConfig)

mod_authnz_ldap (E)

AuthLDAPCharsetConfig *filename*

Pathname of the language to charset conversion configuration files.

AuthLDAPDereferenceAliases   DH (AuthConfig)

mod_authnz_ldap (E)   Always

AuthLDAPDereferenceAliases {Always|Searching|Finding|Never}

Specifies when *mod_authnz_ldap* should dereference aliases.

AuthLDAPRemoteUserAttribute   DH (AuthConfig)

mod_authnz_ldap (E)

AuthLDAPRemoteUserAttribute *attribute*

The value of the specified attribute will be used to set the
REMOTE_USER environment variable. This directive takes precedence
over the AuthLDAPRemoteUserIsDN directive.

AuthLDAPRemoteUserIsDN   DH (AuthConfig)

mod_authnz_ldap (E)   OFF

AuthLDAPRemoteUserIsDN { ON | OFF }

If set to ON, the value of the REMOTE_USER environment variable is set
to the full DN of the authenticated user, rather than to the username
supplied by the client.

AuthLDAPUrl   DH (AuthConfig)
mod_authnz_ldap (E)

`AuthLDAPUrl scheme:host:port/basedn?attr?scope?filter` `[ctype]`

RFC2255 URL specifying the LDAP search parameters and an optional connection type; *scheme* is either ldap or ldaps; *port* defaults to 389 for ldap and 686 for ldaps. Although LDAP allows multiple attributes to be specified in a URL and separated by commas, only the first one is used, and it defaults to uid. *scope* is either one or sub, defaulting to sub. The default filter is objectClass=*.

The optional *ctype* parameter overrides the connection type. It may be NONE for an unsecure connection, SSL for a secure connection on the default ldaps port, or TLS or STARTTLS for an upgraded secure connection on the default LDAP port.

Authentication Phase Directives

This phase is also called the *search/bind* phase, as *mod_authnz_ldap* searches for the username supplied by the HTTP client and attempts to bind to the LDAP server with the resulting DN and the password supplied by the client.

AuthLDAPBindDN   DH (AuthConfig)
mod_authnz_ldap (E)

`AuthLDAPBindDN DN`

Optional DN to use when binding to the LDAP server for the search. If not specified, an anonymous bind is used.

AuthLDAPBindPassword   DH (AuthConfig)
mod_authnz_ldap (E)

`AuthLDAPBindPassword password`

Password to use in conjunction with *AuthLDAPBindDB*.

Authentication Phase Directives

This is also known as the *compare* phase, as many of the authorization rules require LDAP comparisons.

AuthzLDAPAuthoritative   DH (AuthConfig)

mod_authnz_ldap (E)   ON

AuthzLDAPAuthoritative { ON | OFF }

Specifies whether the *mod_authnz_ldap* module is authoritative for authorization or should fall back to other modules on failure.

AuthLDAPCompareDNOnServer   DH (AuthConfig)

mod_authnz_ldap (E)   ON

AuthLDAPCompareDNOnServer { ON | OFF }

If set to ON, DNs are compared on the LDAP server; otherwise, a simple string comparison is done.

AuthLDAPGroupAttribute   DH* (AuthConfig)

mod_authnz_ldap (E)

AuthLDAPGroupAttribute *attribute* ...

Specifies the LDAP attributes that are used to check for group membership. If this directive is not included, then the member and uniquemember attributes are used.

AuthLDAPGroupAttributeIsDN   DH (AuthConfig)

mod_authnz_ldap (E)   ON

AuthLDAPGroupAttributeIsDN { ON | OFF }

If set to ON, the DN of the client is used when checking for group membership; otherwise, the username is used.

CHAPTER 5

Document Metainformation

Once the request URL has been translated and access controls have been applied, Apache determines certain characteristics of the document to be returned, such as the language, content type, character set, and encoding of the document. The content handler and possibly input and output filter chains are also set up at this point (configuration of handlers and filters is covered in the following chapters).

The main module involved in this phase of request handling, apart from the core, is *mod_mime*; other modules set up specialized metainformation. Content handlers may change any of these attributes later.

Note that unless otherwise stated, file extension arguments are case-insensitive and may be specified with or without a leading period (.).

Standard Document Attributes

Four standard document attributes are used for content negotiation. Clients indicate preferences in Accept* request headers, and the attributes of the selected document are used to set response headers.

Content language

> The natural language of the document, such as **en-gb** for British English, **es-mx** for Mexican Spanish, or **zh** for unqualified Chinese. The client's preferences are indicated in the **Accept-Language** header, and the language of the selected document is returned in the **Content-Language** header.

Content type

> The MIME type of the document, such as **text/html** or **image/png**; preferences are indicated with **Accept**, and the document MIME type is returned in **Content-Type**.

Character set

> The MIME character set is also referred to as the character encoding, such as **utf8**, **shift-jis**, or **iso-8859-1**; preferences are indicated with **Accept-Charset**, and the document character set is returned in a **charset** parameter to the **Content-Type** header.

Content encoding

> The encoding of the document, such as **compress**, **deflate**, **gzip**, or **identity**; preferences are indicated with **Accept-Encoding**, and document encoding is returned in **Content-Encoding**.

AddCharset   SVDH* (FileInfo)

mod_mime (B)

`AddCharset charset ext ...`

Maps the specified extensions to the content character set, overriding any existing mappings for the extensions.

AddDefaultCharset   SVDH (FileInfo)

core   OFF

`AddDefaultCharset { ON | OFF | charset }`

Default charset to be added to the **Content-Type** header for responses with a content type of **text/plain** or **text/html**. The value **ON** is equivalent to **iso-8859-1**, while **OFF** disables the functionality.

AddEncoding SVDH* (FileInfo)

mod_mime (B)

`AddEncoding MIME-encoding ext ...`

Maps the specified extensions to the encoding type, overriding any existing mappings for the extensions. Comparison of encodings is performed, ignoring any leading "x-"(which indicates an experimental encoding).

AddLanguage SVDH* (FileInfo)

mod_mime (B)

`AddLanguage MIME-language ext ...`

Maps the specified extensions to the content language, overriding any existing mappings for any of the extensions.

AddType SVDH* (FileInfo)

mod_mime (B)

`AddType MIME-type ext ...`

Adds a mapping from the specified extensions to the MIME type, overriding any existing mappings for the extensions.

DefaultLanguage SVDH (FileInfo)

mod_mime (B) no default language

`DefaultLanguage MIME-language`

Specifies the default languages for files that do not have a language extension configured by the AddLanguage directive. Note that if no default language is specified, files without a language extension have no language attribute.

DefaultType SVDH (FileInfo)

core text/html

`DefaultType MIME-type`

Default content type returned for documents that cannot be typed.

ForceType   DH (FileInfo)
mod_mime (B)

`ForceType MIME-type`

Forces files to be served as a specified MIME type, regardless of file extensions.

ModMimeUsePathInfo   D
mod_mime (B)   OFF

`ModMimeUsePathInfo { ON | OFF }`

If set to ON, the path information part of the URL is combined with the filename when *mod_mime* applies its directives to requests; this means that virtual resources will have metainformation applied based on their extensions. If set to OFF, only the part of a URL that maps to a file or directory will be considered.

MultiviewsMatch   SVDH* (FileInfo)
mod_mime (B)   NegotiatedOnly

`MultiviewsMatch { Any | NegotiatedOnly | Filters | Handlers } ...`

Compatibility: 2.0.26 and later

Influences how the MultiViews feature of *mod_negotiation* behaves. If set to NegotiatedOnly, every extension on files that match the base request must be associated with a content type, character set, language, or encoding. Extensions associated with filters or handlers are not considered for MultiViews, unless Filters or Handlers are specified. The Any option will consider all files, even those with unrecognized extensions.

RemoveCharset   VDH* (FileInfo)
mod_mime (B)

`RemoveCharset ext ...`

Compatibility: 2.0.24 and later

Removes any character set associations from files with the extensions specified.

RemoveEncoding

VDH* (FileInfo)

mod_mime (B)

`RemoveEncoding ext ...`

Removes any encoding associations from files with the extensions specified.

RemoveLanguage

VDH* (FileInfo)

mod_mime (B)

`RemoveLanguage ext ...`

Compatibility: 2.0.24 and later

Removes any language associations from files with the extensions specified.

RemoveType

VDH* (FileInfo)

mod_mime (B)

`RemoveType ext ...`

Removes any MIME type associations for files with the specified extensions.

TypesConfig

S

mod_mime (B)   `conf/mime.types`

`TypesConfig filename`

Filename of the MIME types configuration file, as an absolute filename or relative to the server root directory. The file provides default mappings, from filename extension to content type, that are used if the content type is not set by other means.

Lines in the file should contain a MIME type followed by a list of extensions separated by whitespace. Blank lines and lines starting with a hash sign (#) are ignored.

Automatic Type Determination

The *mod_mime_magic* module provides an alternative way of determining the content type and encoding of files. It works in the same way that the Unix `file` command does: by examining the first few bytes of the file and comparing the data with rules specified in a *magic file*.

MimeMagicFile   SV

mod_mime_magic (E)

`MimeMagicFile` *filename*

Specifies the filename of the MIME magic file and enables the *mod_mime_magic* module. If the filename is not absolute, it is taken to be relative to the server root directory. Note that determining the content type from the magic file can degrade performance.

Document Expiry

The *mod_expires* module supports the generation of `Expires` headers, which inform clients, including proxies, of how long the document contents remain valid and thus how long they may be cached. Expiry times are given as intervals either from the time of the request or from the time the file was last modified. They can be specified either as the letter "A" (for time of access) or "M" (for last modified time), followed by a number of seconds, or in the format:

> *base* [[plus] {*number period-type* ...}]

base may be `access` or `now` for time of access, or `modification` for the last-modified time of the file. Valid period types are: `years` (365 days), `months` (30 days), `weeks`, `days`, `hours`, `minutes`, and `seconds`.

ExpiresActive

SVDH (Indexes)

mod_expires (E)   OFF

ExpiresActive { ON | OFF }

Controls whether HTTP Expires headers are generated for documents in the matching scope.

ExpiresByType

SVDH (Indexes)

mod_expires (E)

ExpiresByType *MIME-type expiry-spec*

Defines how the value of Expires headers are calculated for documents of the specified content type.

ExpiresDefault

SVDH (Indexes)

mod_expires (E)

ExpiresDefault *expiry-spec*

Defines how the value of Expires headers are calculated for documents that do not match any ExpiresByType directives.

Manipulating HTTP Headers

The *mod_headers* module provides the means to manipulate arbitrary request and response headers, while the Apache core provides directives for generation of Content-MD5 and ETag headers.

ContentDigest

SVDH (Options)

core   OFF

ContentDigest { ON | OFF }

Enables or disables the generation of Content-MD5 headers for static documents served by the Apache core module. This header provides an integrity check but imposes a performance penalty on the server as the value is recomputed for each request.

FileETag
SVDH (FileInfo)

core
inode mtime size

FileETag *attribute* ...

Specifies the file attributes that are used to generate the ETag response header field for documents based on files. ETag, or entity tag, values are used in cache management to save network bandwidth. See Table 5-1.

Table 5-1. File attributes used in ETag values

Attribute	Description
inode	inode number of the file
mtime	Date and time the file was last modified
size	File size in bytes
all	All attributes (inode, mtime, and size)
None	No ETag header will be included in the response

Note that if documents are served from multiple servers with mirrored filesystems, then it is best not to include the inode numbers in ETags, as these will probably differ between the servers.

Header
SVDH* (FileInfo)

mod_headers (E)

Header [*cond*] *action hname* [*value*] [*repl*] [early|env=[!]*var*]

Manipulates the HTTP response header named *hname* according to *action*, the values of which are listed in Table 5-2. *cond* may be either onsuccess, in which case only 2xx responses are affected, or always. *value* and *repl* are arguments for the action. The optional final argument either specifies a condition that must be fulfilled for the action to be applied, or is the keyword early, which specifies that the action is carried out at the start of request processing (normally Header actions are applied just as the response is sent out).

Table 5-2. Header and RequestHeader actions

Action	Description
add	Adds the specified header—even if it already exists—which can result in multiple headers with the same name.
append	Adds the specified header if it doesn't yet exist; if it does, the value is appended to the existing header, separated from the current value with a semicolon (;).
edit	If the header *hname* exists, a regular expression search and replace is performed on its value; *value* contains the pattern and *repl* the replacement string, which may contain back-references (Apache 2.2.4 and later).
echo	Request headers that match *hname*, which may be a regular expression, are echoed back in the response headers. This action is not supported by the RequestHeader directive.
merge	Adds the specified header if it doesn't yet exist; if it does, the value is appended to the existing header, separated from the current value by a semicolon (;), but only if the new value doesn't already appear in the header (Apache 2.2.9 and later).
set	The header of the specified name is set. Any previous value is replaced.
unset	The header named *hname* is removed.

The value specified for the add, append, merge, and set actions may contain format specifiers: %% is replaced with a literal percent sign; %t with the time when the request was received, in microseconds since January 1, 1970; %D with the duration in microseconds of the request; %{*var*}e with the value of the named environment variable; and %{*var*}e with the named SSL environment variable.

RequestHeader   SVDH* (FileInfo)
mod_headers (E)

RequestHeader *action hname* [*value*] [*repl*] [early|env=[!]*var*]

Manipulates the HTTP request header named *hname* according to *action*, the values of which are listed in Table 5-2. The behavior is similar to that of the Header directive, except that this directive acts on request headers rather than response headers, the action is normally processed immediately before the handler is run, and the echo action is not available.

CERN Metafiles

Metafiles contain additional metainformation in the form of HTTP headers that are added to the response for a resource. The feature was first implemented in the (now obsolete) CERN web server.

The metafile for a particular resource is found by looking in the subdirectory named by MetaDir, within the directory containing the resource file, for a file with the same name but with the suffix specified by MetaSuffix appended. For example, using the default values, the metafile for index.html would be .meta/index.html.meta.

If a metafile contains a Content-Type or a Status header, then the content type for the document and the response status are set accordingly.

MetaFiles
SVDH (Indexes)
OFF

mod_cern_meta (E)

MetaFiles { ON | OFF }

Enables or disables metafile processing.

MetaDir
SVDH (Indexes)
.web

mod_cern_meta (E)

MetaDir *dir-name*

Name of the subdirectory containing metainformation files.

MetaSuffix
SVDH (Indexes)
.meta

mod_cern_meta (E)

MetaSuffix *suffix*

Filename suffix for metainformation files.

User Tracking

The *mod_usertrack* module enables individual users' accesses to be logged by means of cookies. If a request is received without a tracking cookie, a new cookie with a unique value is set. The cookie value can be included in a log format with the specifier %{cookie}n.

CookieDomain

SVDH (FileInfo)

mod_usertrack (E)

no domain is set

CookieDomain *domain*

The domain name set in the user-tracking cookie. If not set, then no domain is included in the cookie header and the client will associate the cookie with the full domain name of the server.

CookieExpires

SVDH (FileInfo)

mod_usertrack (E)

session lifetime

CookieExpires *expiry-period*

Expiry period set on user-tracking cookies, either as a number of seconds or as a string, such as "1 hour 30 minutes".

CookieName

SVDH (FileInfo)

mod_usertrack (E)

Apache

CookieName *name*

Name of the user-tracking cookie; should only consist of letters, digits, underscores (_), and hyphens (-).

CookieStyle

SVDH (FileInfo)

mod_usertrack (E)

Netscape

CookieStyle *style*

Format used for the Set-Cookie response header field.

Netscape
> The original Netscape cookie syntax. This is the syntax understood by most browsers.

Cookie, RFC2109
> The standard that superseded the original syntax.

Cookie2, RFC2965
> The most recent standard.

CookieTracking SVDH (FileInfo)

mod_usertrack (E) OFF

CookieTracking { ON | OFF }

Enables user tracking by sending a cookie for any request that does not have a user-tracking cookie.

Environment Variables

Apache sets up the standard CGI environment variables and the additional variables listed in Appendix B. Also, variables can be passed from the environment that the server inherits from the invoking shell.

PassEnv SV*

mod_env (B)

PassEnv *varname* ...

Variables to be passed from the server's environment to that of the CGI script.

SetEnv SVDH* (FileInfo)

mod_env (B)

SetEnv *varname value*

Sets the environment variable to the specified value and places it in the environment of the CGI script.

UnsetEnv SV*

mod_env (B)

UnsetEnv *varname* ...

Removes the specified variables from the environment of the CGI script.

CHAPTER 6

Content Handlers

Apache offers many ways of generating content, such as static files, CGI scripts, automatically generated directory indexes, server status pages, and customized error responses. Content is generated by handlers; Table 6-1 lists the handlers provided by the modules distributed with Apache.

Table 6-1. Standard built-in handlers

Handler name	Module	Description
default-handler	*core*	Static content
cgi-script	*mod_cgi*	Content generated by a CGI script
imap-file	*mod_imagemap*	Server-side imagemap file
isapi-handler	*mod_isapi*	Content generated by an ISAPI extension
send-as-is	*mod_asis*	File includes HTTP headers and is sent as-is
server-info	*mod_info*	Generated server configuration information page
server-status	*mod_status*	Generated server status page
type-map	*mod_negotiation*	Content negotiation type map

Apache also provides a filtering mechanism that allows requests to be modified before they are handled and allows the output of the handler to be handled. Filters are covered in the next chapter.

The content handler and any filters that apply are determined as the metainformation for the request is set up.

Handler Configuration

Handlers are named internal functions that generate content. How the content is generated is determined according to the handler or the MIME type that has been set for the resource. If no handler is specified, then a default handler that simply sends the contents of a file as the response is used.

AddHandler   SVDH* (FileInfo)

mod_mime (B)

AddHandler *handler-name ext ...*

Associates the named handler with the filename extensions specified (in addition to any existing association for the extensions).

RemoveHandler   VDH* (FileInfo)

mod_mime (B)

RemoveHandler *ext ...*

Removes any existing handler associations for the specified extensions.

SetHandler   DH (FileInfo)

mod_mime (B)

SetHandler { *handler-name* | None }

Forces all requests in the current scope to be handled by the specified handler. The value None removes the effect of a SetHandler directive in an enclosing scope.

Static Files

Static files are served by the core if the handler is set to default-handler.

The *mod_asis* module provides the `send-as-is` handler to send files that contain static documents, complete with headers. Apache will add a `Date` and a `Server` header to the document, and use the `Status` CGI header, if present, to set the HTTP response code.

Automatically Generated Directory Indexes

If there is no index file for a directory and the `Indexes` option is enabled, a directory listing will be generated. This may be a plain list of filenames or a *fancy index* in which, by default, each line consists of an icon indicating the file type, the filename, the time the file was last modified, the file's size, and a description of the file.

The `IndexOptions` directive controls formatting of the generated listings. The other directives control aspects of the appearance of the lines of fancy indexes, such as header file, stylesheet, icons files, alternative text for the icons, and the descriptions of the files.

IndexOptions   SVDH (Indexes)

mod_autoindex (B)   no options

`IndexOptions {[+|-]option} ...`

Controls the formatting of automatically generated directory indexes. The following options are recognized:

`Charset=character-set`
> Sets the character set of the generated page—default is either UTF-8 or ISO-8859-1, depending on the operating system (2.0.61 and later).

`DescriptionWidth={ n | * }`
> Sets the width of the description column. If specified as an asterisk (*), the width of the longest description is used.

`FancyIndexing`
> Enables fancy indexing.

`FoldersFirst`
> Lists subdirectories before files (2.0.23 and later).

HTMLTable

Uses an HTML table for the directory listing (2.0.23 and later).

IconsAreLinks

Makes each icon a link to the file listed on that line.

IconHeight=*pixels*

If specified, a `height` attribute is generated for the `<img>` element for each icon, allowing browsers to calculate the layout of the page before all of the images have been downloaded.

IconWidth=*pixels*

If specified, a `width` attribute is generated for the `<img>` element for each icon.

IgnoreCase

Sorts names case-insensitively.

IgnoreClient

Ignores all query variables from the client, including the sort order.

NameWidth=*n*

Specifies the width of the filename column in bytes. If *n* is specified as an asterisk (*), the column is automatically sized to the length of the longest filename.

ScanHTMLTitles

Scans HTML files for `<title>` elements and uses the values as the file descriptions.

ShowForbidden

Includes files that are normally hidden because access to them requires authentication or is forbidden.

SuppressColumnSorting

Disable the generation of sortable listings.

SuppressDescription

Suppresses the file description column.

SuppressHTMLPreamble

If a header file is specified with the `HeaderName` and the file contains a valid HTML header, then the generated header will be suppressed and instead taken from the header file.

SuppressLastModified

Suppresses the last-modified date and time column.

SuppressRules

Suppresses the horizontal rules in the fancy index listing.

SuppressSize

Suppresses the file size column.

TrackModified

Returns `Last-Modified` and `ETag` headers for the directory listing, which allows clients to track changes by performing a `HEAD` request. Note that this only works on operating systems that update directory timestamps when the size or timestamps of files within the directory change (2.0.23 and later).

Type=*MIME-type*

MIME content type of the generated page; the default is `text/html` (2.0.61 and later).

VersionSort

Sorts filenames containing version numbers in a natural way.

XHTML

Generated listing page is XHTML 1.0 rather than HTML 3.2 (2.0.49 and later).

AddAlt   SVDH* (Indexes)

mod_autoindex (B)

AddAlt "*string*" *filename* ...

Sets the alternate text for the icon images included for files that match *filename*.

AddAltByEncoding   SVDH* (Indexes)

mod_autoindex (B)

AddAltByEncoding "*string*" *MIME-encoding* ...

Sets the alternate text for the icon images included for files with the specified encoding.

AddAltByType   SVDH* (Indexes)

mod_autoindex (B)

```
AddAltByType "string" MIME-type ...
```

Sets the alternate text for the icon images included for files with the specified content type.

AddDescription   SVDH* (Indexes)

mod_autoindex (B)

```
AddDescription "description" file-pattern ...
```

Sets the descriptive text to display for a file.

AddIcon   SVDH* (Indexes)

mod_autoindex (B)

```
AddIcon { url | alt,url } file ...
```

Relative URL, or ALT text and URL, of the icon to display for files matching the names given. *file* can be a filename extension, a wildcard expression, a partial or complete filename, the string ^^DIRECTORY^^ for directories, or ^^BLANKICON^^ for the blank icon used to line up the columns.

AddIconByEncoding   SVDH* (Indexes)

mod_autoindex (B)

```
AddIconByEncoding { url | alt,url } MIME-encoding ...
```

Relative URL of the icon to display for files whose MIME encoding matches one of those listed.

AddIconByType   SVDH* (Indexes)

mod_autoindex (B)

```
AddIconByType { url | alt,url } MIME-type ...
```

Relative URL of the icon to display for files whose MIME type matches one of those listed.

DefaultIcon

mod_autoindex (B)

DefaultIcon *url*

Relative URL of the icon to display when no other icon is associated with a file's type or encoding.

HeaderName

mod_autoindex (B)

HeaderName

Names the file containing descriptive header text that is inserted at the top of the directory listing. If this is an HTML file, then the appearance of the index can be influenced by BODY attributes, such as BACKGROUND or BGCOLOR.

IndexIgnore

mod_autoindex (B)

IndexIgnore *pattern* ...

Specifies files to be excluded from the directory listing.

IndexOrderDefault

mod_autoindex (B)   in ascending order by filename

IndexOrderDefault *sort-order* *field-name*

Specifies how files should be ordered within the directory listing. *sort-order* may be Ascending or Descending and *field-name* may be Name, Date, Size, or Description.

IndexStyleSheet

mod_autoindex (B)

IndexStyleSheet *url-path*

Specifies the URL of the CSS stylesheet for directory indexes.

mod_autoindex (B)

ReadmeName *filename*

Names the file appended to the end of the directory listing.

CGI Scripts

The CGI interface allows applications to be launched from web servers in a way that is language-independent and portable to most web servers. The downside is the overhead required to launch a CGI script for each request. Embedded interpreters, such as *mod_perl*, avoid this overhead and provide better performance. Other solutions, such as FastCGI and SpeedyCGI, provide a CGI-like environment in a separate process and avoid the cost of initializing an interpreter for each request.

Files are regarded as CGI scripts if the handler is set to cgi-script, and are executed in accordance with the CGI specification. The cgi-script handler is implemented by both the *mod_cgi* and the *mod_cgid* modules—the former module is used with multiprocess MPMs, the latter with threaded MPMs where forking a process is an expensive operation. The modules are identical in configuration and operation.

If the suexec CGI wrapper is properly installed, then Apache will run scripts as the user and group specified with SuexecUserGroup; otherwise, they will be run as the user and group under which the web server child process runs.

Action   SVDH* (FileInfo)

mod_actions (B)

Action { *MIME-type* | *handler-name* } *script*

Script to be invoked if the MIME type or handler matches that of the requested resource.

CGIMapExtension

DH* (FileInfo)

core

CGIMapExtension *program-path ext*

Compatibility: Netware only

Sets the program to handle files with the specified extension.

Script

SVD*

mod_actions (B)

Script *method script*

Script to be invoked if the HTTP request method is the one given.

ScriptInterpreterSource

SVDH (FileInfo)

core

Script

ScriptInterpreterSource { Registry | Registry-Strict | Script }

Compatibility: Windows platform only

Controls how Apache locates script interpreters on the Windows platform. If set to Script, Apache will examine the first line of the script for the name of an interpreter referenced after the #!. If set to Registry, the registry will be searched for an interpreter to handle the extension of the script file. With Registry-Strict, Apache performs a narrower search of the registry.

ScriptSock

S

mod_cgid (B)

logs/cgisock

ScriptSock *filename*

The base filename of the socket to use for communicating with the CGI daemon; the process ID of the server is appended to the filename.

SuexecUserGroup

SV

mod_suexec (E)

SuexecUserGroup *user group*

Compatibility: 2.0 and later

Specifies the user and group that the suexec program should switch to before executing CGI programs or commands executed with the SSI **exec** directive.

Internet Server Extension API

The *mod_isapi* module implements the Internet Server extension API (ISAPI), version 2.0, allowing extensions written for Microsoft's Internet Information Server (IIS) to be run, with some restrictions, on Windows versions of Apache. To associate URLs with this module, the handler should be set to isapi-handler.

ISAPIAppendLogToErrors
SVDH (FileInfo)

mod_isapi (B)   OFF

ISAPIAppendLogToErrors { ON | OFF }

Records HSE_APPEND_LOG_PARAMETER requests to the error log.

ISAPIAppendLogToQuery
SVDH (FileInfo)

mod_isapi (B)   ON

ISAPIAppendLogToQuery { ON | OFF }

Records HSE_APPEND_LOG_PARAMETER requests to the CustomLog %q (query field) component.

ISAPICacheFile
SV*

mod_isapi (B)

ISAPICacheFile *filename* ...

List of files to be loaded when Apache starts and remain loaded until the server is shut down.

ISAPIFakeAsync
SVDH (FileInfo)

mod_isapi (B)   OFF

ISAPIFakeAsync { ON | OFF }

If set to ON, simulates asynchronous support for ISAPI callbacks.

ISAPILogNotSupported

SVDH (FileInfo)

mod_isapi (B)

OFF

ISAPILogNotSupported { ON | OFF }

Logs requests from ISAPI extensions for unsupported features to the error log.

ISAPIReadAheadBuffer

SVDH* (FileInfo)

mod_isapi (B)

49,152

ISAPIReadAheadBuffer nbytes

Maximum size of the read-ahead buffer sent to ISAPI extensions when they are initially invoked. Any remaining data must be retrieved using the ReadClient callback; however, some ISAPI extensions may not support the ReadClient function.

WebDAV

WebDAV is a set of extensions to the HTTP protocol that enables distributed authoring and versioning. It underpins Web Folders and the Subversion version control system.

Dav

D

mod_dav (E)

OFF

Dav { ON | OFF | provider-name }

Controls whether WebDAV methods are enabled for a location.

DavDepthInfinity

SVDH*

mod_dav (E)

OFF

DavDepthInfinity { ON | OFF }

Controls whether PROPFIND requests that include a header "Depth: Infinity" are allowed.

DavGenericLockDB

SVD

mod_dav_lock (E)

DavGenericLockDB filename

Full pathname of the DAV lock database (excluding the extension) used by the generic locking module.

DavLockDB   SV

mod_dav_fs (E)

DavLockDB *filename*

Full pathname of the DAV lock database (excluding the extension) used by the filesystem DAV provider module.

DavMinTimeout   SVD

mod_dav (E)   0

DavMinTimeout *secs*

Minimum lock timeout when a client requests a DAV resource lock.

Server-Generated Status Pages

The server information page provides an overview of the server configuration, including all installed modules and directives. It is generated by the **server-info** handler.

The status page is generated by the **server-status** handler and provides an overview of the current activity of the server.

Note that if either of the *mod_info* or *mod_status* modules are active, they will be available in per-directory configuration files so users with control over those files will be able to publish information about the server.

AddModuleInfo   SV*

mod_info (E)

AddModuleInfo *module text*

Adds the HTML string to the additional information section of the server information display.

ExtendedStatus

	S
mod_status (E)	OFF

ExtendedStatus { ON | OFF }

Controls whether minimal or detailed statistics are maintained for display as a status page. Enabling extended statistics extracts a small performance penalty as additional statistics must be collected.

SeeRequestTail

	S
mod_status (E)	OFF

SeeRequestTail { ON | OFF }

Compatibility: 2.2.7 and later

If set to ON, then the last 63 characters of any long request line will appear in the extended status page, rather than the first 63 characters.

Customized Error Responses

Apache allows the normal hardcoded error response to be replaced with customized responses.

ErrorDocument

	SVDH (FileInfo)
core	

ErrorDocument *error-code* { default | "*message*" | *url* }

Configures the response Apache generates for error responses. The response document can be a message string or the URL of a local or external document. If the local URL refers to a CGI script or SSI document, details of the request can be extracted from the environment.

CHAPTER 7

Filters

Filters are a mechanism introduced in Apache 2.0 to preprocess client POST data before it is seen by the content handler, and to postprocess the output from the handler before it is sent back to the client. Filters can be chained and can modify the metainformation as well as the data itself. They can be used explicitly and are also used internally by Apache, for example, for implementing SSL encryption. Table 7-1 lists the filters provided by standard Apache modules.

Table 7-1. Standard built-in filters

Filter name	Module	Description
DEFLATE	*mod_deflate*	Output compression
INFLATE	*mod_deflate*	Input uncompression
INCLUDES	*mod_include*	SSI processing
SUBSTITUTE	*mod_substitute*	Response body substitutions

Simple Filter Configuration

Filters can be configured statically in *mod_mime*, which may be appropriate if the filtering requirements for a resource always remain the same.

AddInputFilter

SVDH* (FileInfo)

mod_mime (B)   OFF

`AddInputFilter` *filter*[*;filter* ...] *ext* ...

Compatibility: 2.0.26 and later

Maps each of the extensions to the input filter specified in the semicolon-separated filter list.

AddOutputFilter

SVDH* (FileInfo)

mod_mime (B)   OFF

`AddOutputFilter` *filter*[*;filter* ...] *ext* ...

Compatibility: 2.0.26 and later

Maps each of the extensions to the output filter specified in the semicolon-separated filter list.

RemoveInputFilter

VDH* (FileInfo)

mod_mime (B)

`RemoveInputFilter` *ext* ...

Compatibility: 2.0.26 and later

Removes any input filter associations for files with the specified extensions.

RemoveOutputFilter

VDH* (FileInfo)

mod_mime (B)

`RemoveOutputFilter` *ext* ...

Compatibility: 2.0.26 and later

Removes any output filter associations for files with the specified extensions.

SetInputFilter

SVDH (FileInfo)

core

`SetInputFilter` *filter*[*;filter* ...]

Sets the input filters that should handle client requests and POST input for the resource.

SetOutputFilter   **SVDH** (FileInfo)

core

SetOutputFilter *filter*[*;filter* ...]

Sets the output filters that should handle the resource.

Dynamic Filter Configuration

The *mod_filter* module provides a filter framework that allows
output filters to be selected dynamically based on request
header, response header, or environment variable. The
FilterChain directive is used to configure the output filter
chain for the context in which it appears (and for any lower-
level contexts that inherit from that context) with one or more
filter harnesses, each having one or more filter providers, which
are ordinary filters and are registered with the harness with the
FilterProvider directive.

FilterChain   **SVDH*** (Options)

mod_filter (B)

FilterChain { ! | [+|=|-|@]*filter* } ...

Configures a filter chain with filter harnesses declared with
FilterDeclare. An exclamation mark (!) clears the filter chain.

+*filter*
  Adds the filter to the end of the chain

@*filter*
  Adds the filter to the start of the chain

-*filter*
  Removes the filter from the chain

=*filter*
  Replaces the chain with the new filters

FilterDeclare SVDH* (Options)

mod_filter (B)

`FilterDeclare` *filter* [*type*]

Declares an output filter harness; *type* specifies the type of the filter harness:

resource
> Content filter (default)

content_set
> Second level content filter—should not alter the content type

protocol
> Handles protocol between server and client

transcode
> Handles transport-level encoding, such as chunking

connection
> Connection-oriented filtering

network
> Handles the sending and receiving of data to and from the client

FilterProtocol SVDH* (Options)

mod_filter (B)

`FilterProtocol` *filter* [*provider*] *flag* ...

Ensures that filters don't run when they shouldn't and that HTTP headers take account of the effects of the filters. If *provider* is specified, then the flags apply to that provider in combination with *filter*; otherwise, they apply to any provider with *filter*. The valid flags are:

byteranges=no
> Cannot work on byte ranges.

cache=no
> The filter renders the content uncacheable.

change={yes|1:1}
> Indicates that the filter changes the content; if specified as 1:1, the filter does not change the content length.

---

proxy=no

    The filter should not be run in a proxy context.

proxy=transform

    The filter transforms the response in a way that is incompatible with the HTTP header `Cache-Control: no-transform`.

FilterProvider   SVDH* (Options)

mod_filter (B)

`FilterProvider filter provider[{env|req|resp}=]name value`

Registers a provider for the filter; *provider* must be a registered output filter. The provider is invoked if the dispatch criterion is met; this is specified with the last two parameters. *name* is the name of an environment variable, or the name of a request or response header, or the literal string `Handler`; *value* is the value that should be matched. If *value* is prefixed with an exclamation mark, the sense of the test is negated; if *value* starts with one of the prefixes listed in Table 7-2, the test is that indicated; otherwise, a test for an exact match is made.

Table 7-2. FilterProvider test prefixes

Prefix	Test type
$	Substring match
/	Regular expression, delimited by a second /
=	Numeric equality
<	Less than
<=	Less than or equals
>	Greater than
>=	Greater than or equals
*	Unconditional match

FilterTrace   SVD

mod_filter (B)

`FilterTrace filter number`

Sets the level of debug output for the specified filter. By default no debug information is generated.

External Filters

The *mod_ext_filter* module allows external Unix-style filter programs to be defined as Apache filters. Such filters are usually slower than filters implemented as Apache modules, but they can be useful for prototyping.

ExtFilterDefine   S*

mod_ext_filter (E)

ExtFilterDefine *filter param* ...

Defines the characteristics of an external filter; *filter* specifies the name of the filter, which is used in the SetOutputFilter directive. A command line must be specified:

cmd=*command-line*
    The command line to be executed; if this includes spaces, the argument should be enclosed in quotes.

disableenv=*env*
    The filter will be disabled if the environment variable *env* is set.

enableenv=*env*
    The filter will only be enabled if the environment variable *env* is set.

ftype=*filter-type*
    Specifies the filter type. This is specified as a *magic number* with the following meanings: 10 (resource), 20 (content_set), 30 (protocol), 40 (transcode), 50 (connection), or 60 (network).

intype=*mime-type*
    MIME type of documents that should be filtered—if specified, then filtering will be disabled for documents of other types.

mode={input|output}
    Indicates whether the filter is an input or an output filter. Default is output.

outtype=*mime-type*
    MIME type of the output of the filter; by default it is assumed that the MIME type is not changed by the filter.

PreservesContentLength

Indicates that the filter does not change the content length of the document filtered. By default it is assumed that the filter will change the document length.

ExtFilterOptions

D*

mod_ext_filter (E)　　　　　　　　　DebugLevel=0 NoLogStderr

ExtFilterOptions *option* ...

Specifies options for the external filter module:

DebugLevel=*integer*

Level of debug messages generated by the module that should be written to the server error log

LogStderr

Enables logging of messages written by the external filter program to its standard error stream

NoLogStderr

Disables logging of messages written by the external filter program to its standard error stream

Note that debug messages are only logged if LogLevel is set to debug.

Deflate Filter Directives

The *mod_deflate* module implements a DEFLATE output filter and an INFLATE input filter using the zlib data-compression library; the filters provide on-the-fly compression and decompression.

DeflateBufferSize

SV

mod_deflate (E)　　　　　　　　　　　　　　8,096

DeflateBufferSize *nbytes*

Compatibility: 2.0 and later

Specifies the size of the buffer used for compression.

DeflateCompressionLevel

mod_deflate (E)

SV

set by the zlib library

`DeflateCompressionLevel` *level*

The zlib compression level on a scale from one (lowest) to nine (highest). Higher levels consume more CPU. The default is set by the zlib library.

DeflateFilterNote

mod_deflate (E)

SV

`DeflateFilterNote` [Ratio | Input | Output] *note-name*

Records a note that can then be included in a custom log format; the optional first argument indicates whether the note should hold the compression ratio as a percentage (default) or as the byte count of the filter's input or output stream.

DeflateMemLevel

mod_deflate (E)

SV

9

`DeflateMemLevel` *level*

Influences the space/time trade-off of the compression function. Level 1 uses the least amount of memory but is slowest and reduces the compression level; level 9 uses the highest amount of memory but is fastest.

DeflateWindowSize

mod_deflate (E)

SV

15

`DeflateWindowSize` *number*

Controls the compression window size used by zlib. This value can be between 1 and 15; reducing the value tends to reduce the compression ratio.

Server-Side Includes (SSI)

The *mod_include* module implements an INCLUDES output filter that interprets SSI directives embedded within HTML comments in the filtered document. Prior to Apache 2.0, SSI was implemented as a content handler named `server-parsed`; the server still recognizes this handler name and activates the `INCLUDES` filter.

The `Includes` option must be active on the directory containing SSI files for SSI processing to be enabled. The `IncludesNOEXEC` option disables the `exec` command and any file inclusion that would result in the execution of a CGI script.

The following SSI directives are recognized:

`<!--#config attribute=value -->`

Configures aspects of parsing. Valid attributes are shown in Table 7-3.

Table 7-3. SSI configuration attributes

Attribute	Description
echomsg	Message returned if an echo element attempts to print an undefined variable; overrides the `SSIUndefinedEcho` directive (2.1 and later)
errmsg	Message returned if an error occurs during SSI parsing; overrides the `SSIErrorMsg` directive
sizefmt	Format to use for file sizes; either `bytes` or `abbrev`
timefmt	`strftime()` format string used for dates

`<!--#echo encoding=enc var=var -->`

Prints the value of a CGI or SSI variable specified with the `var` attribute, encoded according to the `encoding` attribute (see Appendix B for a list of variables). At the start of the directive, the default encoding is `url` (URL encoding); this may be changed to `entity` (entity encoding) or `none`.

`<!--#exec { cmd=cmd-string | cgi=url-path } -->`

Executes the shell command (using `/bin/sh`) or the CGI script specified.

`<!--#flastmod { file=file-path | virtual=url-path } -->`

Prints the last modification time of the file specified.

`<!--#fsize { file=file-path | virtual=url-path } -->`

Prints the size of the file specified.

```
<!--#include { file=file-path | virtual=url-path } -->
```
Includes the file specified.

```
<!--#printenv -->
```
Prints a list of all variables and their values.

```
<!--#set var=varname value=value -->
```
Sets the value of the variable specified.

```
<!--#if expr="cond" -->
<!--#elif expr="cond" -->
<!--#else -->
<!--#endif -->
```
Defines conditional blocks. The following comparison operators are supported: =, !=, <, <=, <, and >=. Comparisons may be enclosed in parentheses for grouping, prefixed by an exclamation mark (!) to negate the condition, and combined with AND (&&) or OR (||) operators.

mod_include defines a number of additional environment variables, which are listed in Table 7-4. CGI and SSI variables may be interpolated into quoted strings by prefixing the name with a dollar sign ($). The name must be enclosed within curly braces to delimit it, if followed by valid name characters.

Table 7-4. Additional SSI environment variables

Variable	Description
DATE_GMT	Current date and time, expressed in GMT
DATE_LOCAL	Current date and time, expressed in the local time zone
DOCUMENT_NAME	Filename of the requested document, without any leading directory components
DOCUMENT_URI	The %-decoded URL path of the requested document
LAST_MODIFIED	The last modification time of the requested document

SSIAccessEnable

DH

mod_include (B)

OFF

```
SSIAccessEnable { ON | OFF }
```

Enables the -A operator within SSI conditional expressions.

SSIEndTag

mod_include (B)   `"-->"`

SSIEndTag *string*

Compatibility: 2.0.30 and later

String marking the end of SSI elements.

SSIErrorMsg

mod_include (B)   `"[an error occurred... ]"`

SSIErrorMsg *string*

Compatibility: 2.0.30 and later

Sets the message that is output if an error occurs. The full text of the default message is "[an error occured while processing this directive]".

SSIStartTag

mod_include (B)   `"<!--#"`

SSIStartTag *string*

Compatibility: 2.0.30 and later

String marking the end of SSI elements.

SSITimeFormat

mod_include (B)   `"%A, %d-%b-%Y %H:%M:%S %Z"`

SSITimeFormat *string*

Compatibility: 2.0.30 and later

The strftime-style string used to display dates and times.

SSIUndefinedEcho

mod_include (B)   `" (none)"`

SSIUndefinedEcho *string*

Compatibility: 2.0.34 and later

String used when an undefined variable is echoed.

XBitHack SVDH (Options)

mod_include (B) OFF

`XBitHack { ON | OFF | Full }`

Controls parsing of files with content type `text/html`. If set to `ON` or `Full`, files that have the user-execute bit set are treated as server-parsed HTML documents. If set to `Full` and the group-execute bit is set, then the `Last-Modified` HTTP response header will be set to the last-modified time of the file.

Response Body Substitutions

The *mod_substitute* module implements the `SUBSTITUTE` output filter, which provides a mechanism to rewrite the response body on-the-fly in the style of *sed*, the Unix stream editor.

Substitute DH* (FileInfo)

mod_substitute (E)

`Substitute s/pattern/substitution/[flags]`

Compatibility: 2.2.7 and later

Defines a substitution rule; character sequences matching *pattern* in the response body are replaced with *substitution*. The delimiter character does not have to be a slash; the character following the initial `s` is used as the delimiter. Substitution behavior is modified by *flags*, the valid values of which are listed in Table 7-5.

Table 7-5. Substitute flags

Flag	Description
f	Flattens the results of the substitution so that subsequent rules may match the output of earlier substitutions.
i	Applies the pattern case-insensitively.
n	Regards the pattern as a fixed string rather than a regular expression.
q	Does not flatten the results. This is quicker, but later substitution rules may not match (Apache 2.2.9 and later).

CHAPTER 8

Caching

Caching is a technique frequently used to speed up slow operations by storing copies of the resulting data to be used for later operations. In the context of web servers, caching is often combined with proxying, but it can also be used to accelerate accesses to local resources, especially generated documents.

Apache offers two forms of caching: a simple, file-oriented form, and a sophisticated, HTTP-aware form.

Simple, File-Oriented Caching

The *mod_file_cache* module provides a basic caching mechanism that is suited to caching a small set of local, static files that are frequently requested. Two techniques are used: the files can either be opened at server startup and kept open, or they can be mapped into the server's memory space. A cached file is only used if the filename exactly matches a filename from the URL mapping phase.

Both caching techniques use limited system resources and are only suitable for a small number of files. Neither technique will detect whether a file changes on disk; if cached files are updated, then the server should be restarted.

CacheFile   S*

mod_file_cache (E)

CacheFile *filename* ...

The specified files are opened at server startup, and the open file handles are cached.

MMapFile   S*

mod_file_cache (X)

MMapFile *filename* ...

The specified files are mapped into memory at startup.

Intelligent Caching

The *mod_cache* module implements a sophisticated caching mechanism, that can cache local documents as well as documents that are retrieved from remote servers. Storage management is implemented by separate provider modules. Caching is enabled by specifying a URL prefix of documents to be cached and the type of storage to use. Resources that require authorization are never cached. Please refer to the full Apache documentation (*http://httpd.apache.org/docs/*) for information about security considerations.

CacheDefaultExpire   SV

mod_cache (E)   3,600, i.e., 1 hour

CacheDefaultExpire *secs*

Expiry time used for documents that have no expiry time or last modified time.

CacheDisable   SV*

mod_cache (E)

CacheDisable *url-path*

Disables the caching of resources with URLs that start with *url-path*.

CacheEnable   SV*

mod_cache (E)

CacheEnable *cache-type url-path*

Enables the caching of resources with URLs that start with *url-path*, using the storage manager specified by *cache-type* as follows:

disk

> Uses the disk-based storage manager of *mod_disk_cache*

fd

> Uses the file-descriptor storage manager of *mod_mem_cache*

mem

> Uses the memory-based storage manager of *mod_mem_cache*

Full URLs may be used to specify proxied resources that should be cached, if forward proxying is enabled for those resources.

CacheIgnoreCacheControl   SV
                                                                         OFF

mod_cache (E)

CacheIgnoreCacheControl { ON | OFF }

If set to ON, then the server will attempt to serve from the cache requests even if the client specifies a no-cache header value (which normally indicates an end-to-end reload). Resources requiring authorization are not affected by this directive.

CacheIgnoreHeaders   SV*
                                                                         None

mod_cache (E)

CacheIgnoreHeaders { *header* ... | None }

Specifies HTTP headers, in addition to the normal "hop-by-hop" headers, that should not be stored in the cache. The value None indicates that only hop-by-hop headers should be ignored.

CacheIgnoreNoLastMod

SV
OFF

mod_cache (E)

```
CacheIgnoreNoLastMod { ON | OFF }
```

If set to ON, documents without a last-modified date will be considered for caching (the expiration date will either be taken from the Expires header or from the default date specified with the CacheDefaultExpire directive).

CacheIgnoreQueryString

SV
OFF

mod_cache (E)

```
CacheIgnoreQueryString { ON | OFF }
```

Compatibility: 2.2.6 and later

If set to ON, requests are treated as having no query string from a caching point of view—requests are cached even if no expiration time is specified, and a cached copy may be used even if the query string differs.

CacheLastModifiedFactor

SV
0.1

mod_cache (E)

```
CacheLastModifiedFactor factor
```

If a retrieved document does not have an expiry date, then one is calculated by multiplying the age of the document (as indicated by the Last-Modified header) by this factor.

CacheMaxExpire

SV
24

mod_cache (E)

```
CacheMaxExpire hours
```

Maximum period before the server will check with the remote server to determine whether a cached document is still valid.

CacheStoreNoStore

SV
OFF

mod_cache (E)

```
CacheStoreNoStore { ON | OFF }
```

Enables the storage of resources with a no-store value for the Cache-Control header.

CacheStorePrivate

SV

mod_cache (E) OFF

```
CacheStorePrivate { ON | OFF }
```

Enables the storage of resources with a `private` value for the Cache-Control header.

Memory-Based Storage

The *mod_mem_cache* module is a memory-based storage manager for *mod_cache*. It implements the cache types `mem` to store objects in memory and `fd` to store file descriptors for objects.

MCacheMaxObjectCount

S

mod_mem_cache (E) 1,009

```
MCacheMaxObjectCount number
```

The number of entries in the in-memory hash table, which gives the maximum number of objects that can be cached.

MCacheMaxObjectSize

S

mod_mem_cache (E) 10,000

```
MCacheMaxObjectSize nbytes
```

Maximum object size to be considered cacheable.

MCacheMaxStreamingBuffer

S

mod_mem_cache (E)

```
MCacheMaxStreamingBuffer nbytes
```

Maximum size of a response of unknown length that will be buffered before it is decided that the response is too big to cache. By default this is set to the smaller of 100,000 or the value of MCacheMaxObjectSize.

MCacheMinObjectSize

mod_mem_cache (E)

`MCacheMinObjectSize` *nbytes*

Minimum object size to be considered cacheable.

MCacheRemovalAlgorithm

mod_mem_cache (E)

`MCacheRemovalAlgorithm { LRU | GDSF }`

The algorithm used to choose objects to purge from the cache when it becomes full. LRU stands for Least Recently Used; GDSF stands for Greedy Dual Size Frequency, which is an improved algorithm that takes into the consideration of the size of objects and frequency of use.

MCacheSize

mod_mem_cache (E)

`MCacheSize` *kbytes*

Amount of memory to use for caching. This should be larger than the value specified with `MCacheMaxObjectSize`.

Disk-Based Storage

The *mod_disk_cache* module is a disk-based storage manager for *mod_cache*. It implements the cache type `disk`.

Responses are stored in files in a cache directory tree, which is created based on hashes of the cached URLs. The cache is structured as a hierarchy of directories to reduce the number of files in each directory and so reduce the time taken for directory searches. The size of the cache can be managed with the `htcacheclean` program.

CacheRoot

SV

mod_disk_cache (E)

CacheRoot *directory*

Pathname of the top-level cache directory.

CacheDirLength

SV

mod_disk_cache (E)   1

CacheDirLength *number*

Length of subdirectory names.

CacheDirLevels

SV

mod_disk_cache (E)   3

CacheDirLevels *number*

Number of levels in the cache directory hierarchy.

CacheMaxFileSize

SV

mod_disk_cache (E)   1,000,000 bytes

CacheMaxFileSize *nbytes*

Maximum file size to be considered cacheable.

CacheMinFileSize

SV

mod_disk_cache (E)   1

CacheMinFileSize *nbytes*

Minimum file size to be considered cacheable.

CHAPTER 9

Proxying

The *mod_proxy* module adds multiprotocol proxy server capabilities to Apache, allowing documents to be fetched from other servers, which may themselves be proxy servers. As of Apache 2.1, *mod_proxy* provides facilities for connection pooling, and, as of 2.2, for load balancing. Caching functionality was moved out of *mod_proxy* in Apache 2.0 and is now provided by *mod_cache*.

Support for individual protocols is implemented by separate provider modules, as listed in Table 9-1. Proxying of content over SSL/TLS connections requires the support of the *mod_ssl* module.

Table 9-1. Proxy support modules

Module	Protocols supported
mod_proxy_ajp	Apache JServ Protocol version 1.3 (AJP13)
mod_proxy_balancer	Pseudoprotocol used for load balancer groups
mod_proxy_connect	HTTP CONNECT, used to tunnel SSL/TLS requests
mod_proxy_ftp	FTP (supports only GET requests)
mod_proxy_http	HTTP and proxied FTP

Basic Proxy Configuration

A request is deemed to be a proxy request if the hostname in the URL is not one served by the server. Requests can also be rewritten to be proxy requests using the `RewriteRule` directives with the `[P]` flag.

A proxy server can operate in two modes: as a *forward proxy*, where it accepts requests for remote URLs and fetches those resources on behalf of clients; or as a *reverse proxy*, where requests for URLs on the proxy server are mapped to remote URLs, retrieved, and returned to the clients as if they originated from the proxy server itself.

mod_proxy recognizes a number of environment variables that modify its behavior:

`force-proxy-request-1.0`
> Forces proxy requests to be made as HTTP/1.0, disabling HTTP/1.1 features.

`Proxy-Chain-Auth`
> Forwards proxy authentication credentials to the next proxy in the chain.

`proxy-interim-response`
> If set to `RFC`, the proxy forwards HTTP interim (1xx) responses to the client. If set to `Suppress`, such responses are suppressed and a warning logged. If not set, interim responses are suppressed but not logged.

`proxy-nokeepalive`
> Disables persistent proxy connections. Connections to remote servers are closed after each request.

`proxy-sendchunked`
> Allows request bodies to be sent to the origin server using chunked transfer encoding.

`proxy-sendchunks`
> Synonymous with `proxy-sendchunked`.

`proxy-sendcl`

> Adds a `Content-Length` header to HTTP requests that include a body without specifying the length. Such requests have to be buffered to determine their length.

`proxy-sendextracrlf`

> Adds an extra `CR/LF` to the end of proxied requests to compensate for a bug in some browsers.

\<Proxy\> SV*

mod_proxy (E)

```
<Proxy url-pattern >
    ...
</Proxy>
```

Container for directives that only apply to proxied requests matching the *url-pattern*. The pattern may include shell-style wildcards.

\<ProxyMatch\> SV

mod_proxy (E)

```
<ProxyMatch regex >
    ...
</ProxyMatch>
```

Container for directives that apply only to proxied requests where the URL matches the regular expression.

AllowCONNECT SV*

mod_proxy (E)   443 and 563

`AllowCONNECT port ...`

Specifies the remote ports that may be used in CONNECT requests.

ProxyBadHeader SV

mod_proxy (E)   IsError

`ProxyBadHeader { IsError | Ignore | StartBody }`

Compatibility: 2.0.44 and later

Specifies how to behave if a bad response header is received:

IsError

   Aborts the request with a 502 (Bad Gateway) error response

Ignore

   Ignores the line and continues processing

StartBody

   Assumes that the empty line separating headers from the body
   has been omitted, and regards the current line as the start of
   the response body

ProxyErrorOverride

mod_proxy (E)

`ProxyErrorOverride { ON | OFF }`

Compatibility: 2.0 and later

If enabled, then errors from the proxied server (4xx and 5xx status
codes) are intercepted and replaced by error responses from the
proxy server.

ProxyFtpDirCharset

mod_proxy (E)

`ProxyFtpDirCharset charset`

Compatibility: 2.2.7 and later

The character set to be used in HTML directory listings generated
by *mod_proxy*.

ProxyIOBufferSize

mod_proxy (E)

`ProxyIOBufferSize nbytes`

The size of *mod_proxy*'s I/O buffer.

ProxyPreserveHost
SV
mod_proxy (E)
OFF

`ProxyPreserveHost { ON | OFF }`

Compatibility: 2.0.31 and later

If set to ON, the Host header included in the proxy request is taken from the incoming request header, rather than using the hostname specified in the ProxyPass directive.

ProxyReceiveBufferSize
SV
mod_proxy (E)
0

`ProxyReceiveBufferSize nbytes`

Allows the system's network buffer size to be adjusted from the default size to improve throughput. A value of zero indicates that the system default should be used.

ProxyTimeout
SV
mod_proxy (E)
300 seconds, i.e., 5 minutes

`ProxyTimeout secs`

Compatibility: 2.0.31 and later

Sets a timeout on proxy requests.

Proxy Chaining

mod_proxy may be configured to retrieve resources from other remote proxies, as well as to contact destination servers directly.

NoProxy
SV*
mod_proxy (E)

`NoProxy { host | domain | ip-addr | subnet } ...`

Requests for documents from these sites are served directly and not forwarded to a remote proxy server configured with the ProxyRemote directive.

ProxyMaxForwards

SV
-1

mod_proxy (E)

`ProxyMaxForwards` *number*

Sets the `MaxForwards` header on a request—if the value is nonnegative and the header is not already set—which can prevent infinite proxy loops.

ProxyRemote

SV*

mod_proxy (E)

`ProxyRemote` { * | *partial-url* } *remote-proxy*

Defines a remote proxy that should be used for requests for URLs that match *partial-url*, or for all requests if the first argument is *.

ProxyRemoteMatch

SV*

mod_proxy (E)

`ProxyRemoteMatch` *url-regex remote-server*

Defines a remote proxy that should be used for requests for URLs that match *url-regex*.

ProxyVia

SV
OFF

mod_proxy (E)

`ProxyVia` { ON | OFF | Full | Block }

Controls the processing of `Via` headers in chained proxy requests, as follows:

OFF

> No `Via` headers are generated, but `Via` header lines in requests and replies are left.

ON

> A `Via` header is generated for the current host, and `Via` header lines in requests and replies are not modified.

Full

> A `Via` header is generated for the current host with the Apache server version included as a comment field. Existing `Via` header lines in requests and replies are not modified.

Block
> No **Via** headers are generated, and **Via** header lines in requests and replies are removed.

Forward Proxy

Clients are explicitly configured to use a forward proxy. Forward proxies have the potential for abuse and should be protected with access controls, or, if not needed, disabled with **ProxyRequests Off**.

ProxyBlock   SV*

mod_proxy (E)

ProxyBlock { * | *host* | *domain* | *word* } ...

Blocks requests for documents from sites that contain any of the items specified in the list, and returns a 403 (Forbidden) response. Any items that may be DNS names are looked up when the server starts, and the corresponding IP addresses are added to the list. Triggering DNS lookups will slow down server startup.

ProxyDomain   SV

mod_proxy (E)

ProxyDomain *domain-name*

Requests received that contain an unqualified hostname will cause a redirection response to the same host with this domain name appended. This is only useful if the server is serving an intranet.

ProxyRequests   SV
                                                                OFF

mod_proxy (E)

ProxyRequests { ON | OFF }

Enables or disables forward proxy requests.

Reverse Proxy

Reverse proxies, also known as gateways or web accelerators, can enhance security by isolating origin servers from the Web; they can also provide performance benefits, especially when used in combination with caching and load balancing, or by offloading the SSL overhead from backend servers. Reverse proxying is configured with `ProxyPass`.

In reverse-proxy mode, the following headers are added to proxy requests:

`X-Forwarded-For`
> IP address of the client

`X-Forwarded-Host`
> The host requested by the client in the `Host` request header

`X-Forwarded-Server`
> The hostname of the proxy server

The parameters listed in Table 9-2 are used to configure connection pooling (Apache 2.1 and later) and load balancing (2.2 and later). Parameters marked with a star (★) are used on load balancer cluster definitions.

Table 9-2. Proxy connection pooling and load balancer settings

Parameter	Default	Description
acquire		If set, defines the maximum time to wait to acquire a connection from the connection pool; if a connection cannot be acquired, a 503 (Server Unavailable) response will be returned.
flushpackets	OFF	If set to ON, then the module will flush its output after every chunk of data received; if set to auto, then output will be flushed if no more data has been received within the time specified with `flush wait`.
flushwait	10	Time in milliseconds to wait for additional input before flushing if `flushpackets` is set to auto.

Parameter	Default	Description
keepalive	OFF	If set to ON, KEEP_ALIVE messages will be sent to the backend server.
lbset	0	Load balancer set ID.
lbmethod ★		Scheduler algorithm used for load balancing: byrequests (weighted request counting—default), or bytraffic (weighted traffic byte count).
loadfactor	1	Normalized weighted load for a load balancer member (between 1 and 100).
max		Maximum number of connections to keep open.
maxattempts ★	1	Maximum number of failover attempts.
min	0	Minimum number of entries that will be held open to the backend server.
nofailover ★	OFF	If set to ON, load balancer failover is disabled.
ping	0	If nonzero, then an AJP CPING request is sent to the backend server before forwarding the request; the value is the time in seconds to wait for a response (AJP protocol only).
redirect		If set, all requests without a session ID will be redirected to the balancer worker that has route set to this value.
retry	60	Retry timeout in seconds for a worker in the error state.
route		Route of load balancer worker—a value appended to the session ID.
smax		Soft maximum number of connections; connections in excess of smax are subject to time to live. Defaults to the value of max.
status		Initial status of the worker: D is disabled, E is error state, H is hot standby, and S is stopped.
stickysession ★		Name of the backend sticky session identifier (either a cookie name or URL-encoded ID).
timeout		Connection timeout in seconds. Defaults to the value of the Timeout directive.

Parameter	Default	Description
ttl		Time to live in seconds for inactive connections in excess of the value of smax.

ProxyPass   SVD*

mod_proxy (E)

```
ProxyPass [path] { ! | url  {param=value} ... [nocanon] }
```

Maps the remote URL into the local server's namespace, making the proxy appear to be a mirror of the remote server; or, if an exclamation mark (!) is specified instead of a remote URL, requests matching *path* will be excluded from proxying. If the directive occurs within a <Location> container, then the local path is taken from the <Location> argument and should be omitted. Connection pooling parameters from Table 9-2 can be specified.

ProxyPassMatch   SVD*

mod_proxy (E)

```
ProxyPassMatch [regex] { ! | url  {param=value} ... [nocanon] }
```

Compatibility: 2.2.5 and later

Identical to ProxyPass, except that this directive uses a regular expression instead of a simple prefix.

ProxyPassReverse   SV*

mod_proxy (E)

```
ProxyPassReverse [path] url
```

Adjusts URLs in the Location, Content-Location, and URI HTTP headers on redirect responses when acting as a reverse proxy in order to avoid the client becoming aware that resources are mirrored. If the directive occurs within a <Location> container, then the local path is taken from the <Location> argument and should be omitted.

ProxyPassReverseCookieDomain   SVD*

mod_proxy (E)

```
ProxyPassReverseCookieDomain internal-domain public-domain
```

Adjusts the domain in Set-Cookie HTTP headers on redirect responses when acting as a reverse proxy in order to avoid the client becoming aware that resources are mirrored.

ProxyPassReverseCookiePath   SVD*

mod_proxy (E)

ProxyPassReverseCookiePath *internal-path public-path*

Adjusts the path in Set-Cookie HTTP headers on redirect responses when acting as a reverse proxy in order to avoid the client becoming aware that resources are mirrored.

ProxySet   D*

mod_proxy (E)

ProxySet [*url*] {*key=value*} ...

Compatibility: 2.2 and later

Sets connection pooling or load balancer parameters for the specified URL; the parameters are listed in Table 9-2. If the directive occurs within a <Location> container, then the URL is taken from the <Location> argument and should be omitted.

Load Balancing

Load-balancing support is provided by *mod_proxy_balancer* for the HTTP, FTP, and AJP13 protocols. It is configured by defining a load-balancing cluster with a <Proxy> section using the balancer scheme. Cluster members are defined with BalancerMember, and then ProxyPass is used to set up a reverse proxy map targeted to the cluster, as illustrated in the following example:

```
<Proxy balancer://ourcluster>
    BalancerMember http://10.0.0.1/ loadfactor=40
    BalancerMember http://10.0.0.2/ loadfactor=30
    BalancerMember http://10.0.0.3/ loadfactor=30
</Proxy>
ProxyPass / balancer://ourcluster/
```

BalancerMember   D*

mod_proxy (E)

```
BalancerMember remote-url [param=value] ...
```

Compatibility: 2.2 and later

Defines a member of a load-balancing group. Only valid within a
`<Proxy>` section that uses the `balancer` scheme. Parameters specific
to the balancer member can be passed as arguments.

ProxyStatus   SV
                                                                     OFF
mod_proxy (E)

```
ProxyStatus { ON | OFF | Full }
```

Compatibility: 2.2 and later

Displays proxy load balancer status in the *mod_status* status page.
The value `Full` is synonymous with `ON`.

CHAPTER 10

SSL/TLS Support

The *mod_ssl* module adds support for SSL/TLS, which provides the ability to encrypt all data exchanged between the client and server, and to authenticate the server to the client and vice versa.

Note that name-based virtual hosts do not work properly with SSL/TLS because the hostname of the virtual host, taken from the Host HTTP header, is required to locate the appropriate server certificate to set up the connection but is not available until after the secure connection has been established.

Secure Server Options

SSLCryptoDevice S
mod_ssl (E)   builtin

SSLCryptoDevice { *engine* | builtin }

Compatibility: 2.1 and later

With *engine* enables the use of a hardware accelerator board—only available if the SSL toolkit was built with "engine" support.

SSLEngine

mod_ssl (E)

SSLEngine { ON | OFF | Optional }

Enables or disables the operation of the SSL/TLS protocol engine. As of Apache 2.1, the value Optional can be specified to allow clients to upgrade an HTTP connection to TLS (RFC2817).

SSLOptions

SVDH (Options)

mod_ssl (E)

SSLOptions {[+|-]option} ...

Sets various runtime options. The available options are:

StdEnvVars

Enables the creation of SSL-related CGI/SSI environment variables. Disabled by default for performance reasons.

ExportCertData

Creates additional CGI/SSI environment variables to hold the PEM-encoded client and server certificates for the current connection. This is disabled by default as it significantly increases the amount of information put into the environment.

FakeBasicAuth

The Subject DN of the client's certificate is taken as the HTTP Basic authentication username so that standard authorization methods can be used. No password is obtained from the user, but a password of xxj31ZMTZzkVA (the word *password* encrypted) is assumed and should be placed in the user password file.

StrictRequire

Overrides a Satisfy Any setting, so that access control failure by *mod_ssl* is authoritative.

OptRenegotiate

Optimizes SSL connection renegotiation when SSL directives are used in a per-directory context.

SSLPassPhraseDialog

mod_ssl (E)   builtin

SSLPassPhraseDialog { builtin | exec:*program* }

The type of dialogue (built-in or through an external program) to employ for getting the pass phrases for encrypted private-key files.

SSLRandomSeed

mod_ssl (E)

SSLRandomSeed { startup | connect } *source* [*bytes*]

Configures sources for seeding the pseudorandom number generator during server startup or as each new SSL connection is established. The following sources are supported:

builtin
> Internal function that uses the current time, process ID, and a randomly chosen extract of the Apache scoreboard data to seed the generator

file:*name*
> External file, such as the kernel random-number source devices

exec:*prog*
> External program (not recommended for use with connect)

SSLUserName

mod_ssl (E)

SSLUserName *variable-name*

Compatibility: 2.0.51 and later

The SSL environment variable that identifies the user. The REMOTE_USER variable is set to this value, and it is used for logging.

Certificates

Certificates contain the subject's public key, information about the certificate, the identity of the subject and of the issuer (certificate authority or CA), and a digital signature, which is a checksum of the information in the certificate encrypted with the issuer's private key. The validity of the signature can be checked by calculating the checksum and comparing it with the signature decrypted with the issuer's public key. If the issuing CA's certificate is available, then it is used to authenticate the subject. Use of the subject's public key from the certificate enables data to be encrypted so that it can only be decrypted by the holder of the corresponding private key, ensuring secure communication.

Server Certificate

The server certificate is used for the browser to authenticate the server.

SSLCertificateChainFile   SV

mod_ssl (E)

SSLCertificateChainFile *filename*

File containing the certificates of the CAs that form the certificate chain of the server certificate. The certificates stored in this file will not be used for client authentication unless they are also present in the CA certificate file or path.

SSLCertificateFile   SV*

mod_ssl (E)

SSLCertificateFile *filename*

File containing the PEM-encoded certificate for the server. The file may also contain the RSA or DSA private key, which may be encrypted, in which case a pass phrase will be requested at server startup. Both an RSA and a DSA certificate file may be specified.

SSLCertificateKeyFile   SV*

mod_ssl (E)

SSLCertificateKeyFile *filename*

File containing the PEM-encoded RSA or DSA private key for the server (if the private key is not combined with the certificate).

Certificate Authority (CA) Certificates

Certificates for trusted CAs are used to verify client certificates presented to the server.

SSLCACertificateFile SV

mod_ssl (E)

`SSLCACertificateFile` *filename*

File containing concatenated PEM-encoded certificates of CAs whose client certificates are used for client authentication.

SSLCACertificatePath SV

mod_ssl (E)

`SSLCACertificatePath` *directory*

Directory containing encoded certificates of CAs whose client certificates are used for client authentication. The certificate filenames are constructed from hashes of the certificates.

SSLCADNRequestFile SV

mod_ssl (E)

`SSLCADNRequestFile` *filename*

File containing a concatenation of PEM-encoded CA certificates that are used when a client certificate is requested to create a list of acceptable CA DNs to be sent to the client as part of the SSL handshake. These CA names are used by the client to select an appropriate client certificate from those it has available.

SSLCADNRequestPath SV

mod_ssl (E)

`SSLCADNRequestPath` *directory*

Directory containing PEM-encoded certificates that together specify the set of acceptable CA DNs that will be sent to the client when a client certificate is requested. The certificate filenames are constructed from hashes of the certificates.

Certificate Revocation Lists (CRLs)

CRLs are lists of certificates, signed by the CA, that are no longer valid.

SSLCARevocationFile   SV

mod_ssl (E)

SSLCARevocationFile *filename*

File containing the concatenation of all PEM-encoded CRLs of trusted CAs.

SSLCARevocationPath   SV

mod_ssl (E)

SSLCARevocationPath *directory*

Directory containing PEM-encoded CRL files of trusted CAs. The certificate filenames are constructed from hashes of the certificates.

Session Caching

Setting up a secure HTTP connection is time-consuming. *mod_ssl* provides a caching mechanism for session keys to avoid unnecessary session handshakes when a client requests multiple documents in parallel.

SSLSessionCache   S

mod_ssl (E)   none

SSLSessionCache { none | dbm:*filename* | shm:*filename* [*size*] }

Specifies the inter-process SSL session cache DBM file.

none
> Disables the global session cache—not recommended

nonenotnull
> Disables the global session cache but sends a non-null session ID to satisfy buggy clients

dbm:*filename*
> Uses a DBM file—can be unreliable under high load

shm:*filename*[(*size*)]
> Uses a high-performance cyclic buffer within a shared memory
> segment

dc:*socket-path*
> Uses the *distcache* distributed-session-caching libraries

SSLSessionCacheTimeout   SV

mod_ssl (E)	300 seconds, i.e., 5 minutes

SSLSessionCacheTimeout *secs*

Sets the timeout in seconds for the information stored in the inter-
process SSL-session-cache file.

SSLMutex   S

mod_ssl (E)	none

SSLMutex *type*

Specifies the type of lock mechanism used for serializing operations
that have to be synchronized, such as access to the session cache.

none *or* no
> No locking performed. This is the default, but it is recom-
> mended that you change it.

sem
> Uses a semaphore under Unix or a mutex under Win32. This
> lock type provides the best performance, if the operating sys-
> tem supports it.

posixsem
> Uses a POSIX semaphore if the underlying platform supports
> it.

sysvsem
> Uses a System V semaphore if the underlying platform sup-
> ports it.

fcntl:*name*
> Physical lock file, locked with the fcntl() function.

`flock:`*name*

>   Physical lock file, locked with the `flock()` function.

`file:`*name*

>   Physical lock file, using the best file locking implementation provided by the underlying platform. Most portable method.

`default` *or* `yes`

>   Uses the default locking implementation for the underlying platform.

SSL-Based Access Controls

When *mod_ssl* is enabled, access controls can be based on the use of a secure connection, a particular protocol, particular cipher suites, or (using `SSLRequire`) arbitrarily complex criteria.

SSL uses only public key cryptography while establishing a session; symmetric encryption is used thereafter as it is much faster. Cipher suites define the cryptographic algorithms used. These vary in strength and are listed in Table 10-1.

Table 10-1. Cipher suites

Tag	Description
Key Exchange Algorithms	
kRSA	RSA key exchange
kDHr	Diffie-Hellman key exchange with RSA key
kDHd	Diffie-Hellman key exchange with DSA key
kEDH	Ephemeral Diffie-Hellman key exchange (no certificate)
Authentication Algorithms	
aNULL	No authentication
aRSA	RSA authentication
aDSS	DSS authentication
aDH	Diffie-Hellman authentication
Cipher Encoding Algorithms	
eNULL	No encoding

Tag	Description
DES	DES encoding
3DES	Triple-DES encoding
RC2	RC2 encoding
RC4	RC4 encoding
IDEA	IDEA encoding
MAC Digest Algorithms	
MD5	MD5 hash function
SHA1	SHA1 hash function
SHA	SHA hash function
Aliases	
SSLv2	All SSL version 2.0 ciphers
SSLv3	All SSL version 3.0 ciphers
TLSv1	All TLS version 1.0 ciphers
EXP	All export-crippled ciphers
EXPORT40	All 40-bit export ciphers
EXPORT56	All 56-bit export ciphers
LOW	All low-strength ciphers (no export, single DES)
MEDIUM	All ciphers with 128-bit encryption
HIGH	All ciphers that use Triple-DES
RSA	All ciphers that use RSA key exchange
DH	All ciphers that use Diffie-Hellman key exchange
EDH	All ciphers that use Ephemeral Diffie-Hellman key exchange
ADH	All ciphers that use Anonymous Diffie-Hellman key exchange
DSS	All ciphers that use DSS authentication
NULL	All ciphers that use no encryption

SSLCipherSuite

SVDH (AuthConfig)

mod_ssl (E)

`SSLCipherSuite cipher[:cipher ...]`

Colon-delimited string of cipher specifications defining the cipher suite that the client is permitted to negotiate during the SSL handshake. In a per-directory context, it forces an SSL renegotiation. The default is `ALL:!ADH:RC4+RSA:+HIGH:+MEDIUM:+LOW:+SSLv2:+EXP`.

SSLHonorCipherOrder

SV
OFF

mod_ssl (E)

`SSLHonorCipherOrder { ON | OFF }`

Compatibility: 2.1 and later

If set to OFF, then the server's choice of cipher takes precedence; otherwise, the client's choice is used.

SSLProtocol

SV
All

mod_ssl (E)

`SSLProtocol [+|-]protocol ...`

Controls which protocol versions are allowed: SSLv2, SSLv3, and TLSv1. The keyword ALL stands for all protocols. Individual protocol version keywords may be prefixed with a + or - to add or remove a protocol from the list of protocols permitted.

SSLRequire

DH (AuthConfig)

mod_ssl (E)

`SSLRequire expression`

Denies access unless the specified expression is satisfied. The syntax is described by the following simplified BNF grammar:

```
expr ::= "true"  |  "false"
       | expr "&&" expr  |  expr "||" expr  |  "!" expr
       | "(" expr ")"  |  comp

comp ::= word op word
       | word "in" "{" wordlist "}"
       | word "in" "OID(" word ")"
       | word "=~" regex
```

```
        | word "!~" regex

op     ::= "==" | "!=" | "<" | "<=" | ">" | ">="
        | "eq" | "ne" | "lt" | "le" | "gt" | "ge"

wordlist ::= word | wordlist "," word

word   ::= integer | string
        | "%{" varname "}"
        | funcname "(" funcargs ")"
```

The standard CGI variables and additional SSL variables listed in Appendix B may be used with %{*varname*}. Other variables can be used with the syntax %{env:*varname*}.

SSLRequireSSL   DH (AuthConfig)

mod_ssl (E)

SSLRequireSSL

Forbids non-SSL access to the resource.

SSLVerifyClient   SV

mod_ssl (E)

SSLVerifyClient *level*

Level of certificate verification to be performed:

none
> No client certificate required.

optional
> Client may present a valid certificate, which must be verifiable by the server.

optional_no_ca
> Client may present a valid certificate, but it will not be verified.

require
> Client must present a valid certificate.

SSLVerifyDepth

SV
0

mod_ssl (E)

`SSLVerifyDepth number`

Number of CA certificates in the chain of certificates to be followed until a CA certificate is found that is held in the CA certificate path or file. A value of 0 means that only self-signed certificates are acceptable, while a value of 1 means that certificates must be signed by a CA that is directly known to the server.

Proxy Directives

mod_ssl implements direct SSL/TLS support for the proxy modules. By default support is disabled; it needs to be explicitly enabled with `SSLProxyEngine On`.

SSLProxyCACertificateFile

SV

mod_ssl (E)

`SSLProxyCACertificateFile filename`

File containing a concatenation of PEM-encoded certificates, in order of preference, of CAs of the remote servers with which the proxy communicates. Used for remote server authentication.

SSLProxyCACertificatePath

SVDHV

mod_ssl (E)

`SSLProxyCACertificatePath directory`

Directory containing encoded certificates of CAs used for remote server authentication. The certificate filenames are hashes of the certificate The certificate filenames are constructed from hashes of the certificates.

SSLProxyCARevocationFile

SV

mod_ssl (E)

`SSLProxyCARevocationFile filename`

File containing the concatenation of all PEM-encoded CRLs for the CAs of remote servers.

SSLProxyCARevocationPath

SV

mod_ssl (E)

`SSLProxyCARevocationPath directory`

Directory containing PEM-encoded CRL files for the CAs of remote servers. The certificate filenames are constructed from hashes of the certificates.

SSLProxyCipherSuite

SVDH

mod_ssl (E)

`SSLProxyCipherSuite cipher-suite`

Colon-separated string of cipher specifications (listed in Table 10-1, shown earlier) defining the cipher suite to be used for the proxy connection.

The default is `ALL:!ADH:RC4+RSA:+HIGH:+MEDIUM:+LOW:+SSLv2:+EXP`.

SSLProxyEngine

SV
OFF

mod_ssl (E)

`SSLProxyEngine { ON | OFF }`

If set to `ON`, then the SSL/TLS protocol engine is enabled for proxied requests.

SSLProxyMachineCertificateFile

S

mod_ssl (E)

`SSLProxyMachineCertificateFile filename`

File containing the PEM-encoded certificates used when authenticating with remote servers.

SSLProxyMachineCertificatePath

S

mod_ssl (E)

`SSLProxyMachineCertificatePath directory`

Directory containing the PEM-encoded certificates used for authenticating with remote servers.

SSLProxyProtocol

SV
All

mod_ssl (E)

`SSLProxyProtocol [+|-]protocol  ...`

Controls which protocol versions are allowed when connecting to a remote server. The keyword `All` stands for all protocols. Individual version keywords (`SSLv2`, `SSLv3`, and `TLSv1`) may be prefixed with a + or - to add or remove a protocol from the list of protocols permitted.

SSLProxyVerify

SVDH (AuthConfig)
none

mod_ssl (E)

`SSLProxyVerify level`

Level of certificate verification of the remote server to be performed:

none
> No certificate required.

optional
> Remote server may present a valid certificate, which must be verifiable by the server.

optional_no_ca
> Remote server may present a valid certificate, but it will not be verified.

require
> Remote server must present a valid certificate.

SSLProxyVerifyDepth

SVDH (AuthConfig)
1

mod_ssl (E)

`SSLProxyVerifyDepth number`

Number of CA certificates in the chain of certificates to be followed until a CA certificate is found that is held in the CA certificate path or file. A value of 0 means that only self-signed certificates are acceptable, while a value of 1 means that certificates must be signed by a CA that is directly known to the server.

In a server or virtual host context, it applies to the communications with the client browser; in a directory context, it applies to the proxy communications with the upstream server.

CHAPTER 11

Logging

There are two main aspects to logging: recording information about errors and other significant events, and tracking accesses to the web pages served. Other types of log information are more specialized, such as scripting, rewriting, and SSL.

On a busy server, log files grow rapidly and can be rotated in the following ways. You can either rename the current files and restart Apache so that it creates new files. Or you can pipe the log output through an external program that manages log rotation, such as the `rotatelogs` program included in the standard distribution or `cronolog` (*http://cronolog.org/*)—a popular, more sophisticated alternative.

Error Logging

Errors and other conditions are recorded to the error log, support for which is provided by the core. The *mod_dumpio* module adds the facility to record the data received and transmitted by Apache to the error log, which is useful for debugging.

ErrorLog
SV

core   logs/error_log

ErrorLog { *filename* | "|*command*" | syslog[:*facility*] }

Specifies the file for logging error messages. If the argument starts
with a pipe character (|), then it is taken as an executable file that
is spawned and passed error messages on its standard input.

LogLevel
SV

core   error

LogLevel *level*

Controls the verbosity of error logging. Messages will only be logged
that are of a severity of *level* or higher. The log levels are listed in
Table 11-1 in descending order of severity.

Table 11-1. Error log levels

Level	Description
emerg	Emergency conditions signifying the system is unusable
alert	Conditions that signify immediate action is required
crit	Critical conditions
error	Error conditions
warn	Warnings
notice	Normal but significant conditions
info	Informational messages
debug	Debugging information

DumpIOLogLevel
S

mod_dumpio (E)   debug

DumpIOLogLevel *level*

Compatibility: 2.2.4 and later

LogLevel must be set to the level specified here, or lower, for I/O
dumping to occur. In earlier versions, *mod_dumpio* would only
generate output if the log level was set to **debug**.

DumpIOInput

	S
mod_dumpio (E)	OFF

DumpIOInput { ON | OFF }

Compatibility: 2.1.3 and later

Enables the logging of all input.

DumpIOOutput

	S
mod_dumpio (E)	OFF

DumpIOOutput { ON | OFF }

Enables the logging of all output.

Request Logging

The last phase of request processing is request logging. This is normally handled by the *mod_log_config* module, which, as its name suggests, is extensively configurable. Log file entries are configured with format strings that consist of literal text interspersed with format specifiers, as listed in Table 11-2. Multiple log files can be defined for the main and virtual servers.

Table 11-2. Log format specifiers

Specifier	Description
%a	Remote IP address
%A	Local IP address
%B	Number of bytes sent (excluding headers)
%b	Number of bytes sent (excluding headers), or "-" if zero
%c	Connection status
%D	Time taken to serve request in microseconds
%{var}e	Value of environment variable var
%f	Filename
%H	Request protocol
%h	Remote host

Specifier	Description
%{hdr}i	Value of incoming header *hdr*
%I	Number of bytes received, including request line and headers (if *mod_logio* is loaded)
%l	Remote logname from identd (if enabled)
%m	Request method
%{label}n	Labeled note from another module
%{hdr}o	Value of outgoing header *hdr*
%O	Number of bytes sent, including headers (if *mod_logio* is loaded)
%p	Canonical port number of the server
%P	Process ID of the child process serving the request
%q	Query string
%r	First line of the request
%s	Request status
%t	Time formatted as prescribed by Common Log Format (CLF)
%{fmt}t	Time formatted according to *fmt*, a strftime() format
%T	Time taken to process the request
%u	Username presented for authentication
%U	URL requested
%v	Canonical name of the server
%V	Server name according to the setting of the UseCanonicalName directive

If the *mod_unique_id* module is active, the unique identifier for the request can be included with %{UNIQUE_ID}e. Cookies generated by the *mod_usertrack* module can be included with %{cookie}n.

BufferedLogs S

mod_log_config (X)   OFF

BufferedLogs { ON | OFF }

Compatibility: 2.0.41 and later

If set, then the writing of log entries is deferred until accumulated entries could no longer be written in one atomic action. This may enhance performance but risks losing information if the server should crash.

CustomLog SV*

mod_log_config (B)

CustomLog *file-or-pipe* { *fmt-string* | *fmt-name* } [env=[!]*var*]

Adds the named log file using the specified format string or named format. Logging may be conditional if the optional last argument is specified.

IdentityCheck SVD

mod_ident (E)   OFF

IdentityCheck { ON | OFF }

Enables logging of the remote username. If enabled, Apache attempts to retrieve the information from the client machine. Retrieving the information causes delays and the information is often unavailable or unreliable, so except when serving an intranet the feature is best left disabled.

IdentityCheckTimeout SVD

mod_ident (E)   30

IdentityCheckTimeout *secs*

Specifies the timeout for ident requests.

LogFormat SV*

mod_log_config (B)   "%h %l %u %t \"%r\" %s %b"

LogFormat *format-string* [*format-name*]

Without a *format-name*, sets the format for log files created with subsequent TransferLog directives. With a *format-name*, creates a named format that can be used in CustomLog directives. *format-string* describes the format of each log line using the specifers listed in Table 11-2.

TransferLog   SV*

mod_log_config (B)

`TransferLog` *file-or-pipe*

Adds the named log using the format defined by the most recent `LogFormat` directive.

Script Logging

The script logging feature aids the debugging of CGI scripts by collecting the request header fields, any error messages, the response, and all output in one log file. It should normally be turned off as it is meant solely as a debugging feature.

ScriptLog   SV

mod_cgid (B)

`ScriptLog` *filename*

Name of the CGI script error log file. Without this directive, no log file is created.

ScriptLogBuffer   SV

mod_cgid (B)   1,024

`ScriptLogBuffer` *nbytes*

Maximum size of a PUT or POST entity body that is logged without truncation.

ScriptLogLength   SV

mod_cgid (B)   10,385,760

`ScriptLogLength` *nbytes*

Maximum length of the script log file. No more information is logged to the file once this size is exceeded.

SSL Logging

SSL requests are logged to the configured access log—as for normal HTTP requests. The *mod_ssl* module adds a %{*var*}x specifier to add the value of the named CGI/SSI variable to the log format. There is also a %{*function*}c specifier to log an SSL function, as listed in Table 11-3.

Table 11-3. SSL log functions

Function	Description
version	SSL protocol version
cipher	SSL cipher
subjectdn	Client certificate subject DN
issuerdn	Client certificate issuer DN
errcode	Certificate verification numeric error code
errstr	Certificate verification error string

Forensic Logging

The forensic logging module, *mod_log_forensic*, logs each request twice: once before processing the request and again after processing is complete. Each request is identified by a unique ID, either generated by *mod_unique_id* (if that module is loaded) or by this module. The included check_forensic script checks forensic logs for requests that did not complete.

ForensicLog   SV*

mod_log_forensic (E)

ForensicLog { *filename* | *pipe* }

Name of the forensic log file or a command to handle piped log output.

Programs and Modules

The Apache distribution includes a number of support utilities and modules.

Support Utilities

The support utilities, listed in Table A-1, are usually installed in the *bin* or *sbin* subdirectory of the server root directory, but this may vary depending on the distribution.

Table A-1. Programs

Program	Description
ab	ApacheBench—a simple web server benchmarking tool
apachectl	Apache runtime control script
apxs	Apache Extension Tool—used to build Dynamic Shared Objects (DSOs)
dbmmanage	Utility to manage DBM-format user-authentication files
htdbm	Alternative utility to manage DBM-format user-authentication files
htdigest	Utility to manage flat-file user-authentication files for Digest authentication
htpasswd	Utility to manage flat-file user-authentication files for Basic authentication

Program	Description
httxt2dbm	Utility to convert plain text *mod_rewrite* map files to DBM format
logresolve	Utility to postprocess access log files to resolve IP addresses
rotatelogs	Logging filter to rotate log files
split-logfile	Simple perl script to split a combined log file for multiple virtual hosts where the first field is the hostname
suexec	Wrapper program to execute CGI scripts under a different user and group from those under which the server processes run (invoked directly from Apache)

Apache Modules

There are over 80 modules included in the Apache 2.2.9 distribution, as listed in Table A-2. Further modules can be found on the Apache Module Registry (*http://modules.apache.com/*).

Table A-2. Apache modules

Name	Status	Description
mod_actions	B	Executes scripts based on MIME type or request method
mod_alias	B	URL mapping and redirection
mod_asis	B	Canned responses from files that include HTTP headers
mod_auth_basic	B	Basic authentication
mod_auth_digest	E	MD5 Digest authentication
mod_authn_alias	E	Allows creation of derived authentication providers
mod_authn_anon	E	Anonymous authentication
mod_authn_dbd	E	User authentication using relational databases
mod_authn_dbm	E	User authentication using DBM files
mod_authn_default	B	Authentication fallback module
mod_authn_file	B	User authentication using text file
mod_authz_ldap	E	Authentication and authorization with LDAP

Name	Status	Description
mod_authz_dbm	E	Group authorization using DBM files
mod_authz_default	B	Authorization fallback module
mod_authz_groupfile	B	Authorization using plain text group files
mod_authz_host	B	Access control based on client hostname, IP address, or environment variable
mod_authz_owner	E	Authorization based on file ownership
mod_authz_user	B	Authorization of named users
mod_autoindex	B	Automatic directory listing generation
mod_cache	E	Cache handler
mod_cern_meta	E	Support for HTTP header metafiles
mod_cgi	B	Executes CGI scripts directly
mod_cgid	B	Executes CGI scripts via a daemon
mod_charset_lite	X	Character set translation/recoding filter
mod_dav	E	WebDAV support
mod_dav_fs	E	WebDAV filesystem provider
mod_dav_lock	E	WebDAV generic locking module
mod_dbd	E	Framework for supporting SQL databases
mod_deflate	E	Compression filter
mod_dir	B	Mapping of URLs that reference directories
mod_disk_cache	E	Disk-based cache storage manager
mod_dumpio	E	Dumps all I/O to error log
mod_echo	X	Simple echo server
mod_env	B	Passing of environments to CGI scripts
mod_example	B	Sample code demonstrating module API
mod_expires	E	Applies Expires headers to resources
mod_ext_filter	E	External filter module
mod_file_cache	X	Basic file caching module
mod_filter	B	Dynamic filter framework
mod_headers	E	Adds arbitrary HTTP headers to resources

Name	Status	Description
mod_ident	E	RFC 1413 identity lookups
mod_imagemap	B	Server-side imagemap handler
mod_include	B	Processes SSI documents
mod_info	E	Server configuration information
mod_isapi	B	Windows ISAPI Extension support
mod_ldap	E	LDAP framework
mod_log_config	B	Configurable logging
mod_log_forensic	E	Forensic logging of requests
mod_logio	E	Adds I/O byte count fields to *mod_log_config*
mod_mem_cache	E	Memory-based cache storage manager
mod_mime	B	Determines document metainformation
mod_mime_magic	E	Determines document types in the manner of the Unix `file` command
mod_negotiation	B	Content negotiation
mod_nw_ssl	B	SSL/TLS handling for Netware
mod_proxy	E	Proxy/gateway server
mod_proxy_ajp	E	Proxy support module for AJP protocol
mod_proxy_balancer	E	Proxy extension module for load balancing
mod_proxy_connect	E	Proxy support module for CONNECT requests
mod_proxy_ftp	E	Proxy support module for FTP protocol
mod_proxy_http	E	Proxy support module for HTTP and proxied FTP
mod_rewrite	E	Powerful URI-to-filename mapping using regular expressions
mod_setenvif	B	Sets environment variables based on client information
mod_so	E	Support for loading modules at runtime
mod_speling	E	Automatically corrects minor mistakes in URLs
mod_ssl	E	Support for SSL/TLS protocols
mod_status	B	Server status display

Name	Status	Description
mod_substitute	E	Response body substition module
mod_suexec	E	Executes CGI scripts securely via wrapper
mod_unique_id	E	Generates a unique identifier for every request
mod_userdir	B	Supports user home directories
mod_usertrack	E	User tracking using cookies
mod_version	E	Support for version-dependent configuration
mod_vhost_alias	E	Dynamically configured mass virtual hosting

CGI Environment Variables

Standard CGI Variables

Note that variables not defined by the CGI specification are marked with a star (★). In addition, HTTP request header field values are added to the environment with the prefix `HTTP_`, and any hyphens in the header field name are changed to underscores (the `Authorization` and `Proxy-Authorization` headers are omitted for security reasons).

AUTH_TYPE
> Authentication method used (only if request is subject to authentication)

CONTENT_LENGTH
> Length of the entity body (for POST requests)

CONTENT_TYPE
> MIME type of the entity body (for POST requests)

DOCUMENT_ROOT ★
> Value of the `DocumentRoot` directive.

GATEWAY_INTERFACE
> CGI version

PATH_INFO
> URL part after script identifier (if present)

PATH_TRANSLATED
> PATH_INFO translated into filesystem

QUERY_STRING
> Query string from URL (if present)

REMOTE_ADDR
> IP address of client

REMOTE_HOST
> DNS name of client (if resolved)

REMOTE_IDENT
> Remote user ID (unreliable, even if available)

REMOTE_USER
> Name of the authenticated user (only if request is subject to authentication)

REQUEST_METHOD
> HTTP request method

REQUEST_URI ★
> URI of the request from the HTTP request line

SCRIPT_FILENAME ★
> Full pathname of the script

SCRIPT_NAME
> Virtual path of the script

SCRIPT_URI ★
> Full URI of the script (only set if *mod_rewrite* is active)

SCRIPT_URL ★
> URL of the script relative to the server (only set if *mod_rewrite* is active)

SERVER_ADMIN ★
> Value of the ServerAdmin directive

SERVER_NAME
> Hostname or IP address of the server used in the request

SERVER_PORT
> Port number of the server used in the request

SERVER_PROTOCOL
> Name and version of the protocol

SERVER_SOFTWARE
   Server software name and version

UNIQUE_ID ✶
   Token that is unique across all requests (only if
   mod_unique_id is active)

Additional SSL Variables

The *mod_ssl* module adds a number of variables to the CGI/
SSI environment. Many of them contain components of the
DNs of the subject and issuer of certificates used in the SSL
connection. The variable names include the names of these
components, as given in Table B-1.

Table B-1. X.509 DN components

Component	Description
CN	Common name
O	Organization
OU	Organizational unit
L	Locality
ST	State or province
C	Country (ISO two-letter country code)
Email	Contact email address

SSL/TLS Protocol Information

The following variables hold protocol-related information:

HTTPS
   Set to **on** if HTTPS is being used

SSL_PROTOCOL
   SSL protocol version (**SSLv2**, **SSLv3**, **TLSv1**)

SSL_SESSION_ID
   Hexadecimal-encoded SSL session ID

SSL_CIPHER
SSL/TLS cipherspec

SSL_CIPHER_EXPORT
Set to `true` if the cipher is an export cipher, otherwise `false`

SSL_CIPHER_ALGKEYSIZE
Number of cipher bits

SSL_CIPHER_USEKEYSIZE
Number of cipher bits used.

SSL_COMPRESS_METHOD
SSL compression method negotiated

SSL_VERSION_INTERFACE
Version of *mod_ssl* (e.g., `mod_ssl/2.2.9`)

SSL_VERSION_LIBRARY
Version of OpenSSL library (e.g., `OpenSSL/0.9.8g`)

Server Certificate Information

The following variables hold information about the server certificate:

SSL_SERVER_CERT
PEM-encoded certificate (if the `ExportCertData` option is set)

SSL_SERVER_M_VERSION
Certificate version

SSL_SERVER_M_SERIAL
Certificate serial number

SSL_SERVER_A_SIG
Algorithm used for signature of certificate

SSL_SERVER_A_KEY
Algorithm used for public key of certificate

SSL_SERVER_V_START
Start time of certificate validity

SSL_SERVER_V_END
    End time of certificate validity

SSL_SERVER_S_DN
    Subject DN

SSL_SERVER_S_*component*
    Component of server's DN (see Table B-1, shown earlier)

SSL_SERVER_I_DN
    Issuer DN

SSL_SERVER_I_*component*
    Component of issuer's DN (see Table B-1, shown earlier)

Client Certificate Information

The following variables hold information about the client certificate environment variables; they are only set if client authentication is in force:

SSL_CLIENT_CERT
    PEM-encoded certificate (if the **ExportCertData** option is set)

SSL_CLIENT_CERT_CHAIN_*n*
    PEM-encoded certificate *n* in certificate chain

SSL_CLIENT_M_VERSION
    Certificate version

SSL_CLIENT_M_SERIAL
    Certificate serial number

SSL_CLIENT_A_SIG
    Algorithm used for signature of certificate

SSL_CLIENT_A_KEY
    Algorithm used for public key of certificate

SSL_CLIENT_V_START
    Start time of certificate validity

SSL_CLIENT_V_END
    End time of certificate validity

SSL_CLIENT_V_REMAIN
Number of days left of certificate validity

SSL_CLIENT_VERIFY
Validity of certificate

SSL_CLIENT_S_DN
Subject DN

SSL_CLIENT_S_*component*
Component of subject DN (see Table B-1, shown earlier)

SSL_CLIENT_I_DN
Issuer DN

SSL_CLIENT_I_*component*
Component of issuer's DN (see Table B-1, shown earlier)

strftime( ) Time Formats

strftime() is a standard C library function that formats date and time values according to a format defined in a specification string; it is composed of literal text interspersed with the conversion specifiers defined in Table C-1. These format specifiers are used in log format strings and SSI configuration options, as well as to define log file templates for the rotatelogs and cronolog log file rotation programs.

Table C-1. strftime( ) format specifiers

Spec	Description
%a	Abbreviated name of the day of the week
%A	Full name of the day of the week
%b	Abbreviated month name according to the current locale
%B	Full month name according to the current locale
%c	Preferred date and time representation for the current locale
%d	Two-digit day of the month (01–31)
%H	Two-digit hour using the 24-hour clock (01–23)
%I	Two-digit hour using the 12-hour clock (01–12)
%j	Three-digit day of the year (001–366)
%M	Two-digit minutes part of the time (00–59)
%m	Two-digit month number (01–12)

Spec	Description
%p	Current locale's AM/PM indicator
%S	Seconds part of the time (00–61, to allow for leap seconds)
%U	Two-digit week number (00–53, where weeks start on a Sunday and week 1 is the first full week of the year)
%W	Two-digit week number (00–53, where weeks start on a Monday and week 1 is the first full week of the year)
%w	Day of the week (0–6, where 0 represents Sunday)
%X	Preferred time representation for the current locale (without the date)
%x	Preferred date representation for the current locale (without the time)
%Y	Year as a four digit number (including the century)
%y	Year as a two digit number (without the century)
%Z	Time zone abbreviation

HTTP Status Codes

Table D-1 lists the numeric values and names of the HTTP status codes defined in RFC 2616.

Table D-1. HTTP status codes

Code	Name
100	Continue
101	Switching Protocols
200	OK
201	Created
202	Accepted
203	Non-Authoritative Information
204	No Content
205	Reset Content
206	Partial Content
300	Multiple Choices
301	Moved Permanently
302	Moved Temporarily
303	See Other
304	Not Modified
305	Use Proxy

Code	Name
307	Temporary Redirect
400	Bad Request
401	Unauthorized
402	Payment Required
403	Forbidden
404	Not Found
405	Method Not Allowed
406	Not Acceptable
407	Proxy Authentication Required
408	Request Timeout
409	Conflict
410	Gone
411	Length Required
412	Precondition Failed
413	Request Entity Too Large
414	Request URI Too Large
415	Unsupported Media Type
416	Request Range Not Satisfiable
417	Expectation Failed
500	Internal Server Error
501	Not Implemented
502	Bad Gateway
503	Service Unavailable
504	Gateway Timeout
505	HTTP Version Not Supported

HTTP Header Fields

HTTP header fields are defined in RFC 2616 and summarized in Table E-1. They may be categorized as:

Request Header Fields
Contain additional information about the request

Response Header Fields
Contain additional information about the response

General Header Fields
Applicable to both request and response messages

Entity Header Fields
Contain information about the entity body or the resource identified by the request

Table E-1. HTTP headers

Syntax	Category
Accept: *media-types*[;q=*qvalue*][, ...]	Request
Accept-Charset: *charset*[;q=*qval*][, ...]	Request
Accept-Encoding: *enc*[;q=*qvalue*][, ...]	Request
Accept-Language: *lang*[;q=*qvalue*][, ...]	Request
Accept-Ranges: [bytes │ none]	Response
Age: *seconds*	Response
Allow: *method*[, ...]	Entity

Syntax	Category
Authorization: *scheme credentials*	Request
Cache-Control: *directive*	General
Connection: close	General
Content-Base: *uri*	Entity
Content-Encoding: *enc*	Entity
Content-Language: *lang*	Entity
Content-Length: *len*	Entity
Content-MD5: *digest*	Entity
Content-Range: bytes *range/length*	Entity
Content-Type: *media-type*	Entity
Cookie: *name*=*value*[; ...]	Request
Date: *date*	General
ETag: *entity-tag*	Response
Expect: *expectation*	Request
Expires: *date*	Entity
From: *email-address*	Request
Host: *hostname*[:*port*]	Request
If-Match: *entity-tag*	Request
If-Modified-Since: *date*	Request
If-None-Match: *entity-tag*	Request
If-Range: { *entity tag*	*date* }	Request
If-Unmodified-Since: *date*	Request
Last-Modified: *date*	Entity
Location: *uri*	Response
MIME-Version: *version*	General
Max-Forwards: *number*	Request
Pragma: { no-cache	*extension-pragma* }	General
Proxy-Authenticate: *challenge*	Response

Syntax	Category
Proxy-Authorization: *credentials*	Request
Public: *method* ...	Response
Range: bytes=*n*[-*m*] [, ...]	Request
Referer: *url*	Request
Retry-After: { *date* | *seconds* }	Response
Server: *string*	Response
Set-Cookie: *name*=*value*[; *options*]	Response
TE: *coding*	Request
Trailer: *header*	General
Transfer-Encoding: *coding*	General
Upgrade: *protocol* [, ...]	General
User-Agent: *string*	Request
Vary: *header* [, ...]	Response
Via: {[*protocol*/]*version* *hostaddr*[:*port*] [(*comment*)] } [, ...]	General
WWW-Authenticate: *scheme realm*	Response
Warning: *code agent* "*text*" [*date*]	General

Index

Symbols

301 (Moved Permanently) status, 45, 46
302 (Found) status, 45, 46
303 (See Other) status, 45
401 (Unauthorized) status, 64
404 (Not Found) status, 44
410 (Gone) status, 46
502 (Bad Gateway) status, 128

A

Accept header, 53, 79
accept method (AcceptFilter), 21
Accept-Charset header, 80
Accept-Encoding header, 80
Accept-Language header, 53, 80
AcceptEx API (WinSock), 24
AcceptFilter directive, 21

AcceptMutex directive, 21
AcceptPathInfo directive, 44
access control
    authentication, 63
    authentication providers, 66–70
    authorization, 70–74
    LDAP support, 74–77
    non-user-based, 61–66
    SSL-based, 144–148
AccessFileName directive, 10
Action directive, 98
AddAlt directive, 95
AddAltByEncoding directive, 95
AddAltByType directive, 96
AddCharset directive, 80
AddDefaultCharset directive, 80
AddDescription directive, 96
AddEncoding directive, 81
AddHandler directive, 92
AddIcon directive, 96

We'd like to hear your suggestions for improving our indexes. Send email to *index@oreilly.com*.

Related Titles from O'Reilly

Web Programming

ActionScript 3.0 Cookbook

ActionScript 3.0 Design Patterns

ActionScript for Flash MX: The Definitive Guide, *2nd Edition*

Advanced Rails

AIR for JavaScript Developer's Pocket Guide

Ajax Design Patterns

Ajax Hacks

Ajax on Rails

Ajax: The Definitive Guide

Building Scalable Web Sites

Designing Web Navigation

Dynamic HTML: The Definitive Reference, *3rd Edition*

Essential ActionScript 3.0

Essential PHP Security

Flash Hacks

Head First HTML with CSS & XHTML

Head Rush Ajax

High Performance Web Sites

HTTP: The Definitive Guide

JavaScript & DHTML Cookbook, *2nd Edition*

JavaScript Pocket Reference, *2nd Edition*

JavaScript: The Definitive Guide, *5th Edition*

Learning ActionScript 3.0

Learning PHP and MySQL, *2nd Edition*

PHP Cookbook, *2nd Edition*

PHP Hacks

PHP in a Nutshell

PHP Pocket Reference, *2nd Edition*

PHP Unit Pocket Guide

Programming ColdFusion MX, *2nd Edition*

Programming Flex 2

Programming PHP, *2nd Edition*

Programming Rails

Rails Cookbook

Upgrading to PHP 5

Web Database Applications with PHP and MySQL, *2nd Edition*

Web Scripting Power Tools

Web Site Cookbook

Webmaster in a Nutshell, *3rd Edition*